On the Hippie Trail

Avalon Travel
Hachette Book Group
555 12th Street, Suite 1850
Oakland, CA 94607

Printed by RR Donnelley in Thailand, Cyber
First Edition. First printing February 2025.
ISBN 978-1-64171-643-7
Signed Edition ISBN 978-1-64171-679-6
B&N Signed Edition ISBN 978-1-64171-680-2

For the latest on Rick's talks, guidebooks, tours, public television series, and public radio show, contact Rick Steves' Europe, 130 Fourth Avenue North, Edmonds, WA 98020, +1 425 771 8303, RickSteves.com, rick@ricksteves.com.

RICK STEVES' EUROPE
Editor: Gene Openshaw
Photographs: Rick Steves and Gene Openshaw
Maps: David C. Hoerlein

AVALON TRAVEL
Managing Editor: Madhu Prasher
Associate Managing Editors: Jamie Andrade, Sierra Machado
Copy Editor: Maggie Ryan
Proofreader: Elizabeth Jang
Production & Typesetting: Bookish Design, Alvaro Villanueva
Cover Design: Faceout Studio, Spencer Fuller
Maps: Kat Bennett

For a peek at Rick's original hand-written journal and more back story on this adventure, go to www.ricksteves.com/hippietrail.

On the Hippie Trail

Istanbul to Kathmandu
and the Making of a Travel Writer

Rick Steves

Contents

Preface

In the spring of 1978, I was a 23-year-old piano teacher, newly graduated from the University of Washington with a history degree, and traveling whenever I could. With 50 wonderful students, I made enough money to spend my summers in Europe, and I fully expected to be a piano teacher for the rest of my life.

But Europe is the wading pool for world exploration, and I was aching to dive into the deep end. My travel dreams were taking me east...to a tantalizing adventure called the "Hippie Trail."

This overland trek—three thousand miles from Istanbul to Kathmandu—promised a once-in-a-lifetime journey through mysterious lands. The route echoed the fabled Silk Road of medieval Marco Polos, adventurers who set off for the "exotic East" and returned with fabulous wealth and fantastic tales.

By the 1960s, this route was attracting a new breed of traveler... young backpackers. Hippies. And when the Beatles famously visited the Maharishi, India became the next frontier, a place where young Westerners could find themselves and their purpose in life. By the time I graduated from college a decade later, hundreds of thousands of backpackers had crossed into India from the West.

I'd been on the verge of taking this trip for two years, but it was scary. I kept booking flights and then finding excuses to cancel, put off India, and do Europe again. But that spring, everything aligned, and I found the perfect travel partner for the adventure of a lifetime.

I teamed up with my school buddy Gene Openshaw, who'd

backpacked around Europe with me in 1973, the summer after our high school graduation. We sketched out a rough itinerary. From Europe, we'd journey to Istanbul, traverse the arid expanses of Turkey, Iran, and Afghanistan, and then cross the Khyber Pass into Pakistan, ultimately arriving at our goal: India and Nepal, including the ultimate mecca of freakdom, Kathmandu.

Back then, India seemed like the edge of the world to me: a magical land of strange gods, dangerous bacteria, golden temples, holy beggars, and hashish. Information was scarce and unreliable. Most travelers just winged it, sharing lessons and warnings from their experiences on the road.

We packed our small rucksacks with what we guessed we might need. We had minimal clothes but plenty of medicine: antibiotics, malaria pills, and iodine drops for our water. We had cameras with enough film to last the trip—if we stuck to our nine-shots-a-day allotment. Finally, we bought a big, fold-out map of the entire 3,000-mile route—our only solid information for this journey into the unknown.

I also packed a journal—a hard-bound empty book ready to collect all my travel memories. I was determined to chronicle the trip, grabbing a stream-of-consciousness-parade of impressions, and I did—writing a thousand words a day.

After the trip, this journal was packed away, never read...forgotten for 42 years. Then, stuck at home during the pandemic, I stumbled across it. And as if on an anthropological dig into my own past, I entered the world of 23-year-old me and relived my coming-of-age trip.

The journal you're about to read has been lightly edited by my Hippie Trail partner, Gene (who became my frequent collaborator in the decades since). With Gene's help, I've condensed some of the more mundane and redundant entries—transportation logistics, meals, waking, sleeping, and hurried trips to the toilet—and rearranged a few itinerary details for better flow and readability. But we are determined to share a candid, unvarnished snapshot of our trip, and we've been careful not to make me sound older, wiser, or more culturally sensitive than I was at the time.

Ready for the adventure of a lifetime? Stow away with me now as Gene and I travel from Europe to Kathmandu. The date is July 14, 1978, the first day of our trip. I open my empty notebook, pull out my cheap Bic pen, and write the very first words…

The Trip — July 13 to Sept 8, 1978

July 13	Travel to Frankfurt	July 29	Meshad – Herat
14	Meet Gene in Frankfurt	30	Herat, Afganistan
15	Train: Germany – Belgrade	31	Herat
16	Belgrade – Plovdiv	August 1	Bus: Herat – Kabul
17	Plovdiv, Bulgaria	2	Kabul
18	Plovdiv	3	Kabul
19	Istanbul	4	Kabul – Rawalpindi, Pakistan
20	Istanbul	5	Rawalpindi – Lahore
21	Bus through Turkey	6	Lahore – Amritsar, INDIA!
22	Bus through Turkey	7	Jammu – Srinagar, Kashmir
23	Bus Erzurum – Iran	8	Srinagar
24	Tehran, Iran	9	Srinagar
25	Tehran	10	Srinagar – Gulmarg
26	Teheran	11	Gulmarg – Nagin Lake
27	Bus Teheran – Mashad	12	Nagin Lake
28	Meshad	13	Srinagar

August 14 Fly: Srinagar - Delhi

15 Delhi

16 Delhi

17 Delhi

18 Delhi - Tansen, Nepal

19 Tansen - Pokara

20 Pokara

21 Pokara

22 Pokara - Katmandu

23 Katmandu

24 Katmandu

25 Katmandu

26 Katmandu - Varanasi

27 Varanasi

28 Varanasi

29 Agra

August 30 Agra

31 Jaipur

Sept 1 Jaipur - Delhi

2 Delhi

3 Delhi

4 Delhi

5 Fly: Delhi - London

6 London

7 Train: London - Frankfurt

8 Fly: Frankft - SEATTLE

Good trip - thats all
I got to say.

56 days
10 countries
countless miles
jillions of experiences
and memories

Rick Steves
Gene Openshaw
9/8/78

Nineteen hundred and seventy-eight was the big
year. At least at the time, Rick Steves felt
he was doing something big. Having finished school
after 18 seemingly endless years the end did come,
the ___ ___ ___ what would follow. The only
___ ___ do was to take a trip - a

___ ___ that a trip was a noble
___ ___ wise investment of time
___ ___ maybe he just had nothing
to do with his time and money and
___ Seattle was good - but for no more
nine months out of twelve.
___ all things to waste, time was the worst
___ Europe, even wasted time is put to use.
___ ___ that Rick saw in Europe was the
___ ___ answer to his fear of a
___ at home.
___ trips ___ ___ ___ much
___ ___ the
___ ___ ___
___ that it was ___
___ ___
___ ___ learned in his head for ___ Finally

Leaving Europe

July 14

July 18

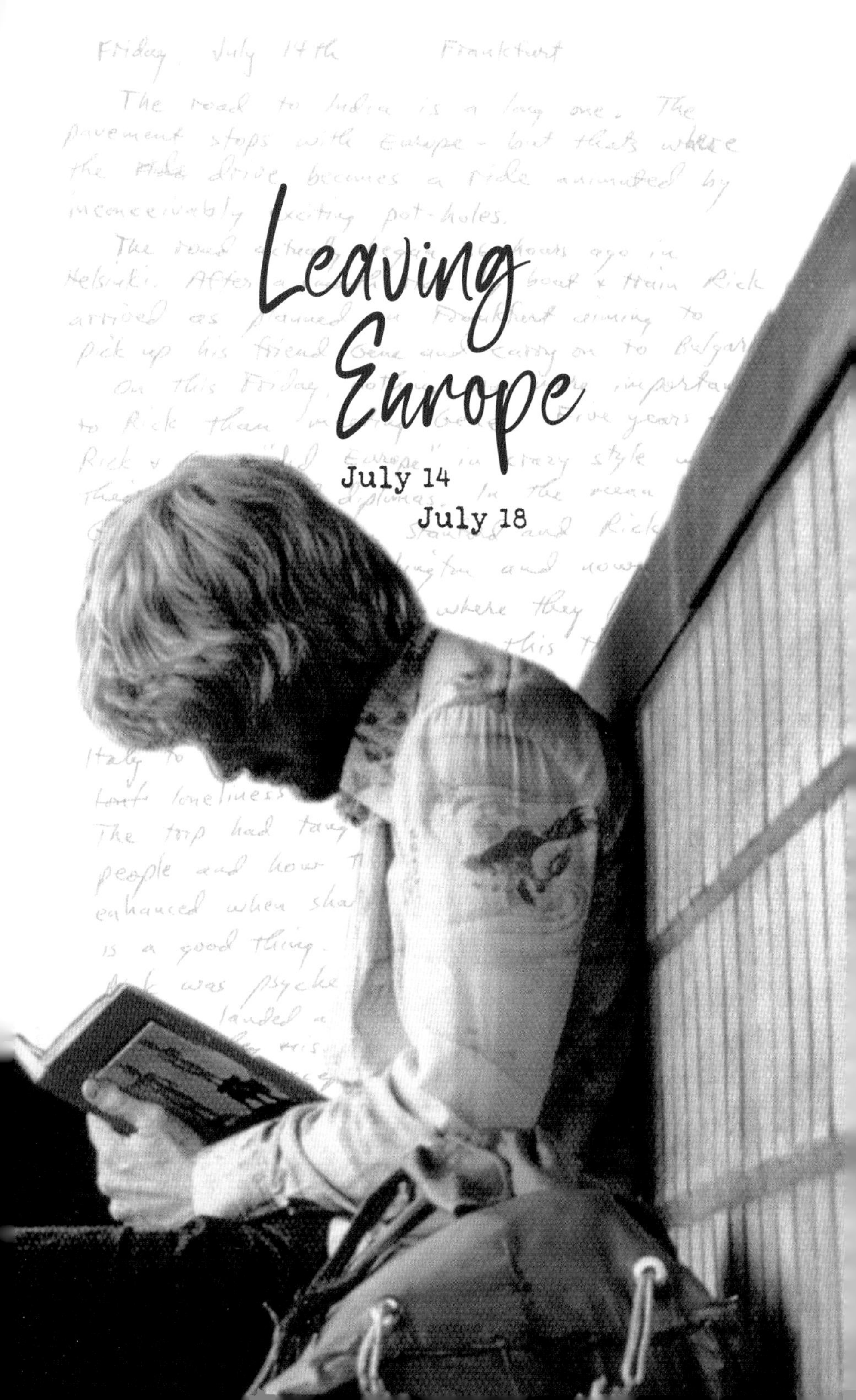

*Journaling diligently, I filled my
empty book with my Hippie Trail tales.*

Nineteen hundred and seventy-eight was the big year. At least at the time, Rick Steves felt he was doing something big. Having finished school after 18 seemingly endless years the end did come. He couldn't imagine what would follow. The only natural thing to do was to take a trip - a long one.

Rick believed that a trip was a noble adventure and a wise investment of time and money but maybe he just had nothing better to do with his time and money and life in Seattle was good - but for no more than nine months out of twelve.

Of all things to waste, time was the worst and in Europe, even wasted time is put to use. The comfort that Rick saw in Europe was the ~~apparent of youth~~ answer to his fear of a wasted summer at home.

After eight trips, Europe had lost much of its magnatism and, refusing to accept the fact, it took one final six weeks on "The continent" to prove to him that it was time for something new. Europe was a well-worn pair of shoes - very comfortable - but lacking soul.

India had burned in his heart for years. Finally the plans were ~~laid~~ made and that's where he was heading. Wide-eyed anticipation of totally new cultures, unforgetable experiences, exposure to life from a bizarre + almost exotic angle filled his spirit. An acceptance of the frustrations, sweat, sickness, sleepless nights, fears + hardships was an integral part of this package deal. A package deal that no one could open and Rick could have it - by travelling through it.

Leaving Europe

Gene's plane landed at 9:10, and I was there at the airport waiting. Somehow, we missed each other as I witnessed every reunion except our own. What a frustrating feeling to watch that electric door open a hundred times and see no familiar face. Waiting like a puppy, the door would open, I'd look for Gene, and see someone else. After an hour, I had Gene paged, but no sign of him.

Bad thoughts traveled through my mind. What if something happened? What if I was destined to spend the next eight weeks alone? Tail between my legs, I returned to Frankfurt's train station to our backup meeting place—lucky Track 13. And that's where Gene was waiting for me.

We were both so happy to meet up. Having already traveled Europe for six weeks this summer, too often in the company of loneliness or someone who was little better, I've learned the value of good people and how the value of good things is enhanced when shared with good people. India is a good thing. Gene is "good people." The table is set…and I'm hungry.

✻   ✻   ✻

We boarded the first train to Yugoslavia, en route to Istanbul. As we rolled through the German countryside, we quickly got down to business. We pulled out our big map of the Hippie Trail and laid it across the seats. There it was—3,000 miles from the edge of Europe to Kathmandu. We went over each country on the road ahead and talked about what little we knew about them. Turkey—chaos. Iran—repression. Afghanistan—tribesmen with rifles. Pakistan—mosques. India—beggars and holy cows. And finally, Nepal—the backpacker's dream of gentle people, high mountains, and high tourists.

All night and the next day were spent on the train. We spent a crowded night not sleeping well. The ride through the lush Austrian countryside was punctuated by nibbling, snoozing, and taking in the views. As the sun rose, I watched peasant families working

Even as a young bloke,
I preferred the non-smoking car.

On the train to Plovdiv, Bulgaria

together with the scarecrows in the fields. We read, played back-gammon on Gene's mini-board, munched, and snoozed some more. We knew this was just the first of many long rides between here and India.

Talking with Gene—of girls, life directions, big decisions, and old friends—seemed to speed the train along. Gene had just graduated from Stanford in Comparative Religious Studies, so he was looking forward to seeing Asia's variety of religions: Islam, Hinduism, Bud-dhism, and Sikhism. With my degrees from the University of Wash-ington in European History and Business Admin, I was excited to get beyond "the West."

We both were excited and a bit scared. A jaded-sounding British guy on the train told us about the risks of crossing Middle Eastern borders where you might get framed for smuggling drugs. He said politics in Iran and Afghanistan were getting hairy, and we might get caught up in some revolution. He wondered for us: Were we ready for the horrible scenes of poverty? And did we have enough money ourselves to even survive the trip?

And we talked about one more thing: would we sample the hashish that we'd heard was as common as dysentery on the fabled trail? We'll see.

Our final dinner on that first train was just lovely: bread and cheese, cabbage, and warm milk in a box that bragged it will never go bad. Sipping it, we agreed it'll never go good either.

The train pulled into Belgrade at 10:00 p.m. We felt we deserved a bed. But the chase for sleep began with hotels (too expensive), then private pensions (still too much), and finally the parks—perfectly within our budgets, but crawling with Yugoslavian policemen.

Retreating back to the train station, we came up with a brilliant idea: find a train car that was going nowhere and sack out in it. We found a car that looked like it hadn't moved in weeks, and within moments we had found the sleep we craved.

Kabam! Lurching forward, the unthinkable happened. Our train jolted into motion and, suddenly, it was going somewhere! Fast as possible, we packed up and watched helplessly as the lights of downtown Belgrade faded and the train lumbered through the night.

Just outside town, it slowed for a small station. Panicked, we figured it was now-or-never. I tossed my rucksack before me and jumped out onto the deserted cement platform. Gene followed, but the train had picked up speed, and he tumbled wildly into the dark. Rushing to his side, I helped him up, and we surveyed the situation. Happily, bruises and scuffs were the only results.

The lone station master, lantern in hand, came over to inspect the Americans who had just dropped into his sleepy station. He let us sleep in the waiting room and, after all that crazy adventure, I was not about to turn down a safe, warm, and free night's sleep. But I lay there haunted by the thought that, in our haste, we could have easily leaped into a pillar, been thrown back onto the train...and died... before we even got out of Europe.

Returning to Belgrade, we caught a train that was actually going somewhere we wanted to go: to see my friend Svetoslav in Bulgaria.

There were no seats left, but we found a spot in the aisle with a fold-down stool and a good window. A Turk with a pile of suitcases provided us with a handy table. The train rolled out, we laid a tiny tablecloth on the top suitcase, and cracked open some never-go-bad milk and cookies. Everyone enjoyed us—like two accidental comedians on the train.

The hours passed slowly, but I didn't really mind—I knew this was only the first small part of a very long journey. The border crossing was typically hassled, but after weathering the stern police, we were successfully into the Communist world. Welcome to Bulgaria.

For me lately, the Iron Curtain opens and closes every year. And in Bulgaria, with Svetoslav and the Tanchevas, it's like I have family. To save a few bucks, I'd purchased tickets only to Sofia, planning to fake our way a few hours farther to Sveti's hometown of Plovdiv. Sofia came and went while we—riding farther than our ticket covered us—sat casually on a big Turkish suitcase, playing backgammon, and hoping they wouldn't check our tickets.

Tension mounted as the conductor neared. Acting nonchalant, like he'd already checked us, didn't work. And he said the word we didn't want to hear: "tickets." Our back-up plan: fake like we didn't realize we had "missed" our stop. Relishing my role as the stupid American tourist, I really played it up. Oh, how I was so upset! The conductor saw a golden opportunity to cash in on this and was trying to charge $25, but I was too distraught! Finally, he began to think this crazy American was funny. After much sweet-talking, he waived our penalty and insisted that we get off the train at the next stop—Plovdiv. As we stepped off—exactly where we wanted to be—I was honored to receive an imaginary Oscar for my acting from Gene.

Now on our own behind the Iron Curtain, we were hoping to be met by a familiar face—my friend Svetoslav. Seeing nothing but a few uniformed soldiers in the strangely quiet station, we thought maybe Svetoslav would be outside the station. Nothing. I studied the map and set out to find his address. We had to be very sneaky as he was not allowed to have Western guests. On the quiet, dark street we walked, feeling the tense excitement of being the forbidden fruit in a socialist country.

Then a whispering voice broke the rhythm of our footsteps: "Rick! Rick!" I told Gene, "Ignore him and just keep walking." We followed the dark figure until, finally, we felt safe enough to acknowledge each other. Svetoslav's warm handshake couldn't begin to express our happiness to be together again.

Sveti's father, Datko, waited nearby in their "Polsky Fiat"— a cheap communist car made in Poland from worn-out factory parts and painted shades of Tupperware. Throwing our rucksacks in, we headed off. Meeting like this was risky for the Tancheva family. But Datko appreciated the value of this courageous parenting for his son and daughter. To have western guests is both a treasured experience and a serious offense. Our packs were left in the car in case snoopy neighbors saw luggage brought in indicating we were spending the night.

We entered their apartment, where a happy reunion was waiting: Sveti's mom (Miko), sister, and Grandma were all there just like they have been for my last four visits. After a nice meal and catching up came the next priority: showers and laundry. Then we climbed under hand-woven blankets of Albanian wool and slept very well.

※　※　※

This day was for relaxing and just enjoying everyone's company. For me, "Bulgaria" is just this one warm, happy family. They barely spoke English, but, after so many summer visits in a row, that wasn't necessary.

Hospitality flowed in many forms, and the most tangible was food. Miko plied us with meat and cheeses, bread, soup, hot milk with sugar, stuffed peppers, pork chops, boiled potatoes, wine, and a local liquor. And the true delicacy: American Coca-Cola—which in Bulgaria is considered the ticket to an amazing time.

Datko, Gene, and Sveti—hiding behind house plants. Entertaining Westerners in your home was a dangerous move in communist Bulgaria.

It's only day two, in Bulgaria, and, realizing "we can't even read the letters here," it occurs to us that we're really in for an adventure. In the 40 years since, Gene and I have co-authored about a dozen guidebooks and two books about European art.

There was good conversation and trading of news. They are my window on the East, and I am their window on the West. For Svetoslav and his freedom-starved family, my annual visits are a highlight of the year.

Gene and I had smuggled in some forbidden Western fruit as gifts: a Texas Instruments calculator, blue jeans, and a Beatles album. These things cost me $40 in America, but their value in Bulgaria is incredible—about six-weeks' wages. It made me feel very good to give such valuable presents as thanks for their boundless hospitality. It's because of our friendship, after repeated visits, that I know Bulgaria far deeper than as a mere tourist.

Then—after another bottle of Coke and some Beatles (of course)—we all took a walk around Plovdiv, a lovely city. Wide, clean, pleasant walking malls are lined by typical socialist-type stores. Only the government can advertise, and it exercises that right liberally, going through tons of red paint. A military band plays patriotic and folk songs in the park. Next to the fountain, men gather to talk sports and whisper politics. Knowing the plainclothes policeman in their midst is monitoring their discussion, they stick to soccer.

We visited the monument to the "liberation of 1945." ("Yeah," Sveti said, "liberation from Hitler to Stalin.") Datko bought us ice cream while we struggled to spend our Bulgarian money, which will be worthless once we leave the country. (I have a theory that while the French calmed the hungry masses with subsidized bread, the Communist governments of Eastern Europe distract revolutionaries with great and cheap ice cream.) We discovered that capitalists in Bulgaria are treated to special prices. When Datko asked the price of a train ticket to Istanbul he was told $11. When I went to buy it, it was $16.

At the Bachkovo Monastery, Datko treated everyone to a local favorite—lamb's head. Ears, teeth, eyeballs, and all. They taught us how to eat it. The tongue and eyeballs were supposed to be best.

19

Datko left only the bones and eyelashes on his plate. The brain was hard to swallow, but it made a fun meal, and I pocketed some teeth for souvenirs.

As darkness fell, they took us to the summer open-air theater for a movie. "But Sveti, we don't speak Bulgarian." "It's ok, just his face will make you laugh." It did.

International trains are routinely hours late. Datko phoned to check on the arrival time. We were having such a good evening together, we hoped it was delayed. But, sadly, our train to Istanbul was on time. We gathered our stuff, plus the wonderful goodies bag Sveti's mom prepared for us (stuffed peppers, a cake, and a freshly baked pod of sunflowers), then hustled to the station.

It's always difficult to leave Plovdiv. We boarded the train, slammed down our window, leaned out as far as we could and waved and blew kisses to our wonderful Bulgarian family as the train rolled us away. This was the last oasis. From now on, we were on our own. Heading east from Bulgaria, it occurred to me that, between here and the end of our journey, I knew not a soul.

The train was packed. We enjoyed the little fold-down seats in the aisle as well as the view out the aisle window, had a good conversation with two Iranians, as, like sardines in a tin, everyone made themselves as comfortable as possible. We hit the Turkey border crossing in the middle of the night. Surprisingly, our American bags weren't even touched, but the poor Iranians had everything sifted through and had to pay the guard a curious tax of two new shirts.

All in all, things couldn't have gone smoother, and with the first light of the new day, we were well into Turkey, free from the hassles of socialist Bulgaria, and falling into the arms of Turkish chaos.

Lamb's head…
In Bulgaria there's
nothing but the best
for out-of-town guests.

refused to get up and said that he had
three friends who were in the bathroom
who had the vacant seats. The 2 other
men, Iranians, were ready to let us in and
apologysed for the Turk. Rick & Gene enjoyed
the view out the aisle window and had
a good conversation with two Iraqis for about
an hour and then broke in on the comfortable
threesome. Like sardines everyone made themselves
as comfortable as possible. One thought sat in
every mind - the border crossing.

This was Rick's 4th Turko-Bulgarian
crossing. Each one was in the middle
night and very very long. The
and one man of

Wednesday   July 19th   Istanbul

I actually slept through the morning and felt
rested upon arrival in crazy Istanbul. Today was
for business - change money, buy a bus ticket to
Tehran, get an Iranian visa, find a hotel.

Feeling right at home I walked up to
my favorite st___ and checked into my regular
hotel. Again ___ A little bit cocky I expected
people to reme___ ___ remembered
them. I didn't ___ ___ the room, I just
___ ___ good

Turkey

July 19
July 23

*Wandering the streets of Istanbul
can be endlessly entertaining.*

Istanbul is normally a finale—my favorite place to finish a European adventure. But this time, rather than a finale, this teeming metropolis is a springboard for more...for India. In Istanbul life just carries on—day after day, the same dusty human pack-horses, the same small boys selling Marlboro cigarettes, the same go-easy guys sitting on piles of tires. Old, retired human pack-horses walk around bent as if still bearing their loads. Just walking around is an experience, and you can't help but become swallowed up in the earthy atmosphere.

But first, business. Gene and I set off to change money, which was a challenge since few banks here accept traveler's checks. The nice thing was that we enjoyed a recently much-improved exchange rate that makes Turkey fantastically cheap. Next, we took in our passports to get an Iranian visa. Then, feeling right at home, I walked up my favorite street and checked into my regular hotel, the Agan Hotel.

A little bit cocky, I expected people to remember me since I remembered them. I didn't even check out the room, I just took what they offered, confident that it would be as good as last year's. As it was too early to check in, we left our bags and headed out...happy to settle in later.

Finally, we took care of our most important order of business: to buy a bus ticket to Tehran. We expected to pay $20, but the going rate was $30-40. Oh well—at least that gets us halfway to India. This would be a two-day bus ride, and comfort was of the utmost importance. We went to the most highly recommended company, Mihan Tours, which advertised: "Big new Mercedes buses—very comfortable." They were so smooth and businesslike in the ticket office, we felt confident that we were with the right company. We booked good seats—numbers 21 and 22 on what promised to be a lovely bus ride.

Now, with our chores taken care of, we were free to enjoy the sights of Istanbul. We visited the Blue Mosque where I saw the same old guy with no legs selling postcards I saw last year...still warming the same steps. We treated ourselves to some *sütlaç* (rice pudding) and cherry juice, and then went back to our hotel to relax.

The room was simply lousy. The shower only trickled, the lights didn't work, and cockroaches flourished. My shoes earned a new nickname: "the roach-stompers." You just stomp and drag across the carpet leaving only a dark smudge—a fate too good for any cockroach found in my hotel room. Worst of all, the toilet didn't flush—it just runneth over. We called for help and what we got was a "new" room that was just the same except the lights worked and the toilet flushed.

Knowing the long road we had ahead of us, Gene and I had promised to treat ourselves to a Turkish *hamam*. A complete Turkish bath and massage is an experience everyone should have, and no one can forget.

Feeling really naked (we had to leave everything, including our money belts, in the little booth) and wrapped only with a towel, we were led into a steamy world. My unshaven Turk said, "okay, *merhaba*," and put me belly-up on the big, round, marble slab, where I was allowed to lie, sweat, look up at the cloudy sun rays spraying through the little holes in the domed roof, and worry about the body-ripping massage I was about to get. I prayed that my joints would all survive.

Then with a loud slap in my chest, he landed on me like a beast and worked me over good. He was a credit to his gender. Smashing and stretching each of my tight muscles, I was in lovely pain. It hurt

Many hotels on the Hippie Trail came with dirt floors and no glass in the windows. When I complained about a dirty sheet, the hotelier apologized and turned it over.

but, in a strange way, I wanted it—just with no lasting damage. Then came the joint stretching. He flipped me over, face down. Bouncing my feet to my back, walking on me, cracking my neck with surely enough power to break it, I'd call the massage an all-out attack. At one point, I realized my left cheek and ear were pressed against the wet marble with the rest of my body at the mercy of my masseuse and, a few feet in front of me was Gene, all wrapped up in the same agonizing pretzel, right cheek and ear pressed against the wet marble. Looking at each other, we were providing the whole ordeal with a soundtrack of constant grunting and groaning.

For the final rinse cycle, they washed and scrubbed us by a hot fountain. When they were through with us, we were totally relaxed... and relieved to be uninjured.

Rested and ready to go for an evening stroll, we plunged into the Turkish bustle, wide-eying our way down to the waterfront, where the Galata Bridge was full of cute Turkish girls—still teeny-bopper-giggly in their 20s. I can't get enough of Istanbul's churning, busy waterfront. We bought fried fish and a hunk of bread right off a fisherman's dinghy which somehow didn't spill its flaming grill as it slammed with the chop against the dock.

Climbing up through the "new town," we passed a street soccer game and neared the top of the hill where we ascended the Galata Tower for a fantastic view of the Golden Horn, Bosphorus, and a sprawling metropolis with millions of people where Asia meets Europe. Gene and I gazed eastward across the water and said to each other, "Asia."

The sun was setting, and we returned to our hotel to have a bite of Miko's Bulgarian cake and stomp a few roaches. We organized and cleaned our packs for tomorrow. I intended to go back outside, but after a shower, I was so comfortable on the bed I never got back up.

At least until 3:00 a.m., when our toilet began to overflow.

Our bus ride to Iran started on an ominous note. The passengers crushed in to grab their seats on the bus to Tehran, and we scoffed at them. Knowing we had reserved seats 21 and 22, we saw no reason to rush on. We took our breakables and what we'd need for the journey into our day bags and heaved our rucksacks to the man standing on top of the bus. They disappeared under a canvas. Last on, we worked our way down the aisle and we realized why the crush: our seat reservations were meaningless.

We took what was left—the last two seats. They were jerry-rigged onto the back of the last row of normal seats over the rear stairwell. They collapsed forward when someone came in the rear entrance but didn't recline back like the others for sleeping. Oh well. It's just 63 hours.

We bounced slowly out of Istanbul, and, taking stock of the situation, we found little to cheer about. The driver looked like a crazy Barbary pirate, complete with scars, a hairy open chest, mustache, and bandana. The #2 man was a half-wit with grotesque pockmarks disfiguring his face. Our window didn't open and was covered with an old, dirty eagle decal. The wheel casing just in front of us cut down legroom and made the ride extra noisy and bouncy. The engine just behind us was hot, smelled, and rumbled constantly. Our reading lights didn't work, and my seat came complete with a sharp point and nasty, exposed screw. Cigarette ashes blew straight into me from nearby smokers, and the cover of the aisle

29

An American was big news in eastern Turkey. When people stared, I assumed they were waiting for entertainment. So, I'd sing. (My go-to was "Huggin' and Chalkin'" by Hoagy Carmichael.)

light crashed to the floor just as we crossed the bridge over the Bosphorus and entered Asia. Cuss this tour bus. Only 62 hours to go.

Gene and I passed time expertly, playing word games, trivia, telling stories, having heavy discussions, reading, and singing old songs. Whenever I'd stand up to stretch my crunched legs, I'd see the pirate spot me in his rear-view mirror and yell, "Mister! Sit down!"

The bus was filled with an interesting group of people. Gene and I were the only Americans. We got talking to a couple of Spaniards who had lots of experience traveling outside Europe. Four or five British, two Belgian, some French, a couple of Basques, a rotund Russian emigre living in Chicago, an Iranian student, and some Muslim women with children rounded out the bus. Compared to everyone else, I think we seemed quite green to this kind of travel.

The lack of any reliable travel information for this Istanbul-Kathmandu trip troubled me. I literally went through the entire bus borrowing whatever anyone had to read up on the trip—even if in German or French. I studied it all. British travelers had the only real "guidebook" for the route, a staple bound collection of travelers' notes called "The BIT Guide: Overland to India." I had plenty of time to read the entire thing, taking lots of notes. I remember how the Brits just kind of tossed it to me like an old magazine and then how I treasured it. The information I gleaned was a windfall.

When it was time to think about sleeping, we cracked open our Bulgarian gift of cognac. At first, I hated the powerful stuff, but I grew bolder and bolder. The Iranians gave us a big glass of Scotch to speed us along. We finished the whole bottle of cognac and were so drunk I couldn't believe it. I never enjoyed a night bus ride so much in seats that didn't recline.

When we had finished off everything, Gene had to take a pee. I'll never forget him—desperate for relief—filling the cognac bottle in the crazy back seat of that crazy bus. I topped it off and we screwed the cap back on, put it gently in the garbage, and slept like babies as we rumbled through Turkey.

∗ ∗ ∗

The "Pirate" (our driver) suddenly started screaming. I snapped awake just as the bus was grinding over the curb and crashing to a noisy stop. Things went flying everywhere (though luckily the human luggage stayed put). Smoke billowed out from our end of the bus. I thought we were on fire and thoughts of how terrible this could be raced through my woozy head.

The pock-faced half-wit had just taken over and couldn't have been driving for more than a minute when he lost control, and we crashed through the median. We all filed out to inspect the damage as the cold Anatolian wind blew fiercely. The bus didn't look too bad, but it was hung up on the two-foot-high curb. The pirate was screaming at the half-wit, while Turkish grease monkeys climbed under the rear end.

We spent the next hour building rock bridges so our Iranian leaders could work the bus out of this jam. Slowly it rocked back onto the road, and we limped into the next town to get it fixed.

No one thought this would be a quick stop. While we waited for the mechanics to repair the bus, the next six hours were spent drinking tea, snoozing, washing under a hose, and getting to know our fellow passengers. We all agreed that the four Iranian crew members were wild and crazy, and, as we had seen, only one could drive a bus. So, the pirate would have to be driving the rest of the long haul alone.

It was becoming apparent—this was to be no 63-hour ride, but the beginning of an odyssey, and we would just have to ride it out.

Finally, the pirate yelled what must have been "all aboard" in Turkish, and we continued eastward.

With smoke, sparks, and screams,
I was jolted awake as our bus ran
off the road and ground to a halt.
We spent the better part of a day
hanging out while the bus was
repaired.

Our seats were folded out over the stairwell in the back of the bus…and unlike every other seat on the bus, they didn't recline. We called our bus driver "The Pirate" and our very survival was in his hands.

We drove through spectacular high country, but not making very good time. The roads were bad, our pace was slow, and by late that night, we were way behind schedule—somewhere in the middle of Turkey and still far from Iran. Very stiff, I stood up to stretch and got eye contact with the pirate in his mirror. As if on cue, he yelled again "Mister! Sit down!" Stopping at a village near Sivas, the driver and his cronies took their time over dinner and got involved in a Henry Fonda movie that was playing on Turkish TV.

Just when we hoped to move on, the pirate suddenly announced—we were staying here.

Gene and I were put in a hotel with the two Belgians in a prison-like, four-bedded room. We grabbed a few hours sleep while those who slept on the bus had a terrible night dealing with the resident half-wit, some horny Turks, and corrupt police looking for trouble.

Rudely awakened for the second morning in a row, I was shrieked out of bed by the crazy pirate and scolded all the way back to the waiting bus. We were late. I was nearly hurled by my collar as I got in but managed a cheery "good morning" to the gang on board.

At first it seemed the pirate was anxious to get going, but after just an hour we suddenly made a breakfast stop—a lengthy one—and we knew that today our tyrannical driver was in no hurry. Then the road got bad, and we were still far from anywhere.

At mid-morning, we stopped by a riverside, and the pirate stripped to his underpants. With soap in hand, he went for a bath and swim. Then like a wild kid, he rolled in the sand for some reason and reentered the river. Then he urged everyone into the river, saying, "No clean, no Tehran." We were slow to catch on, but soon all the men were running around in underpants and floating down the refreshing river. I washed myself and my dusty clothes and dried off in minutes. It felt great.

By now, we had given up hope of any great progress, and our driver was just going to enjoy himself along the way.

Turkey

By late afternoon, we were in Erzurum—barely halfway to Tehran. Our packs were thrown down from the roof, and we were told to find a hotel and report back at 5:00 tomorrow morning.

We wandered about Erzurum for a few hours, checking out a lovely mosque, staring back at lots of curious people with a tough history etched onto their faces, and having a meager bite to eat.

Our no-frills, 35-lira room was moderately bug-free and quiet, although there was no water anywhere, and the place was generally filthy. The toilet was a hole in the floor.

That evening, our room became the meeting place for the English-speaking hippies. We all shared some food that we'd gathered in town—food we thought would be safe to eat. The mood was one of helpless and pessimistic frustration. Our Spanish friends, who seemed to know a lot, worried that our driver and crew might try some kind of funny business, like demanding more money to go on.

We all wondered when we'd get to Tehran—or if.

* * *

By 5:00 we were underway again. The pirate seemed determined to make good time today, and we ripped through the wild east-end of Turkey, making only a quick mid-morning breakfast stop. Feeling very dominated by our boisterous driver, I scored a point with him by offering him a piece of our breakfast watermelon. He said, "Thank you very much. Ok! Allah! Sit down!"

By 10:00, we were approaching the border. Everyone was concerned about the Turkey-Iran border crossing, and rightfully so. The BIT guide explained how it's famous for drug arrests, tearing apart cars, and numerous other hassles. As instructed, Gene and I checked our packs very carefully to make sure that nobody had "planted" anything in them and then kept them safely on our laps.

Passing an endless line of delayed trucks, we came to the check-point and began the long journey through the customs building. All sorts of people were working their way across one way or the other. We filled out forms, waited for body searches that never came, and showed our passports at several points.

We thought we were done, when we were stopped again and went through the luggage check. Everything was unloaded off the roof and searched. One of our wheels was even checked.

Finally, after four long hours at the border, we rolled under the "Welcome to Iran" sign and passed from the omnipresent gaze of Turkey's Atatürk to that of Iran's divine Shah. We set our clocks ahead two hours for Iran time and were cleared to enter.

The pirate was really moving now. I think he wanted to get into Tehran only 24 hours late.

The Iranian countryside was dramatic and I took plenty of pictures. With 14 rolls of film, 36 shots in a roll, and 55 days of travel, I stayed within my limit of about 9 shots a day—and Iran was worth every one.

By 10:00 pm, we were in Tabriz—just in time to witness the armored riot squads ready themselves for student trouble. Iran under its Western-backed dictator, the Shah, is quite repressive. And torture and firing squads don't go over very well with the young generation of any country.

We all worried we'd have to make another overnight stop in Tabriz. But instead, we were stopping to pick up a second driver. We happily said goodbye to the pock-faced half-wit and were soon speeding on a good road straight through toward Tehran.

Now everyone's spirits picked up—this journey would be over by sunrise. The Spaniards sang and clapped *La Bamba,* the Russian did opera, while the little smiley Iranian boy directed with a cigarette. Then the pirate turned the wheel over to his new driver, washed his feet, spritzed everyone with rose water as he pranced down the aisle, made up his bed under the bus's back window, told us to shut up, and went to sleep.

Faddi, Abe's sister came by + everyone else left. Gene was sleeping in the living room + Abe asked him if he wanted a Pizza. What a silly question. Gene had an omelet while Abe ran out + picked up three Iranian Pizzas. Italy is a very long way away.

Abe taught me some fancy backgammon, beating me 3 times very quickly and then we checked on Gene. _____ a fever + was quite down. We _____ the pharmacy and for a minute if _____ that he might have cholera _____ in Turkey but Gene's shots were _____. We gave him some pill to bre_____ fever and then all went to bed _____ waiting till morning to decide if _____ put or go on to Te_____ _____king I woul_____ back _____ for_____

Thursday, July 27th   Tehran-Meshad

    We were up at 5:00 and Gene felt
better. Packing quickly we had cake + coffee
+ Abe drove us down to the bus station.
Goodby dear friend + giver of fun + comfort.
        ... met our Spanish friends from the
            ... ran trip and boarded the bus
            ... he long day's ride to Meshed.
            ...e pulled out. About 40 Muslim
            ...to the ... place and us
            ...who were just curious enough to
            ...   ... The first six hours
            ...etely. The... was quiet, friendly,
            ... driver was safe + steady, stopping
            ...nd the scenery was dramatic.
        ...   ...through a high rugged mountain
pass ...   ...t the the highest mountain
in ...
    The ...   ...ed the Rolling Stones on
their ...   ...e read, enjoyed the
scenery ...   ... friends ...

Iran

July 24
July 28

I loved my trusty Pentax K1000.
We traveled with 36-shot rolls of film
in canisters and, packing light, we
had a strict daily ration of shots
so we didn't run out before
the trip was over.

Arriving in Tehran, it felt great to get off that bus...
even though my body ached from neck to tailbone. We said goodbye
to our bus mates, took a picture of the pirate, and stumbled off. After
four nights and three days, we had traveled from Istanbul to Tehran.
That's 1,500 long miles down—just 2,000 more to Kathmandu.

I was beginning to get a little down. I wondered if all this was
worth it. In my mind a conflict simmered. I would never be satis-
fied until I had traveled overland from Europe to India and Nepal.
But I also didn't want to endure six weeks of hell just to spend
a fortune to fly back home. A persistent siren in my head whispered:
It's not too late to turn back... Fortunately, Gene was strong in that
moment, and pepped up my spirits.

We set off into Iran's capital city. Tehran is huge (4 million
people), busy, sprawling, and very hard for me to get oriented in.
Just taking care of business was a lot of work. We got $100 US
cash for emergencies and bribes that we anticipated but hoped we
wouldn't need on the road to India. For the visa into Afghanistan
we had to leave our passports and three photos at the embassy to
pick up later. Now for the problem we didn't anticipate: there was
a big religious festival in Mashhad, Iran's most holy city and our next
destination, and the buses and trains were all booked solid for days.
We considered flying over it or hitchhiking, but finally we booked
a bus to halfway there, hoping to just fake our way on to Mashhad.

Hoping to boost our spirits, we went out for a soak in a public
bath, but I got in an argument with the guy who was already

charging us double the Iranian price and wanted to charge even more for soap. Of course, I'm rich compared to him and I'd hardly notice the gouge. But it was a matter of principle and I walked out. We bought a street-side dinner of cucumber, boiled eggs, and a hot potato with Cokes, then went off in search of a hotel.

Amir Kabir is the cheapo hotel district where you're bound to run into anyone heading down the Hippie Trail to India. We bumped into many people from our bus ride. Hidden behind piles of tires and greasy auto parts are gross little hotels, and we found a terrible one for 400 rial, or $6. I think it was the worst ever for me, but I have a hunch I'm just getting more sensitive to filth, bugs, broken windows, and cigarette butts stuck in sooty holes in the hotel walls lit by bare-dangling bulbs.

There we sat. Sweltering under a sheet for protection from the bugs, I felt just one step above animal level and worried that I was becoming like the other cheap, hip, road-to-India travelers running around in sweaty underpants and bare feet, who lived in their cave-like rooms like quiet animals and didn't care.

Screeching buses and screaming boys woke us at 4:30 and broken sleep was the best I could get after that. Gene got sick during the night. I don't know what hit him, but something sure did. He rallied enough to move on.

We checked out of our hole-tel, not trusting it enough to leave our bags there, and sought out a slightly better one, a big, cheap hotel called Amir Kabir. We were wait-listed but left our packs in case a room opened up.

Gene wasn't right and he decided to rest in a park for a few hours while I explored the bazaar.

I walked and walked. To survive the barrage an American tourist with a fancy camera and short pants receives, you have to build a hard shell around you. You can step out and make fun things happen. But when things get too heavy, you must be able to pull

Boys build brooms
in the local bazaar.

back inside and mentally repel the onslaught—the grabbing hands, mothers holding babies while they crap in a corner, fleeting "Hello Misters," and the heat, dust, and puddles of muck that only beggars can ignore. It's kind of like putting your head under water—you can do it, but only for so long.

I stepped into a mosque—a cool refuge from the hubbub of life on the street. But while locals came here for calm and community, I felt out of place—like I came from a different planet.

At a museum, I met a nice British girl who was flying home tonight. I felt a little envy. England sounds so cool, refreshing, enjoyable, and easy right now. Once again, I thought: For some reason, I am putting myself through this ordeal and I want to accomplish it. If I don't make it to India, I'll never be content. It will always bug me, and I'll probably end up on this same road on some later "vacation."

We spent a few hours simply wandering. Just being on the streets was an experience. I was looking for postcards and there are very few in Tehran. I also needed something to make my stomach feel good, take care of my thirst, and give me energy. A hard-boiled egg and a 7-Up did the trick. Dirt abounds in Tehran and to eat food with nothing else is quite a trick.

Meeting up with Gene again, we were both exhausted, but we still had a lot of business to take care of: try to buy bus tickets to Mashhad, pick up our Afghan visas, confirm our hotel for the night, and look into Pakistani visas.

We started heading for the Pakistan embassy but got turned around. We tried pulling ourselves out of our confused state by buying a map of Tehran so this huge city might make some sense. But it's difficult when each new mayor decides to change all the street names. After an hour of wandering, we were completely lost, standing on a busy traffic-choked streetcorner with our map out. It must have been 100 degrees.

We never found the embassy but that really didn't matter—we hit the jackpot by meeting a wonderful guy who stopped to help us with our map. When he found out we were Americans he said, "Hey, come have a cup of coffee with me." He was so innocent and happy sounding that we couldn't turn him down. What a lucky break. He introduced himself as Abbas—"or Abe, to Americans."

❊   ❊   ❊

Abe apologized for his messy flat as he fixed us a sandwich, fruit, and a cold beer. He had a gorgeous little apartment and a lifestyle that was royal compared to the common masses filling the streets like we saw in Amir Kabir.

Abe learned English from an American family, picked up Spanish because of his fanatical love for Spanish music, and put everything together to get a job for the government heading a translating department. When he was refused a raise, he was allowed to work part time for whole pay. Continuing that game masterfully, he's now making good money and working about an hour a day!

Abe is quite a playboy. His dates are usually in the afternoon because Iranian girls are watched very closely by their parents, and they rarely live anywhere but at home until they are married. That wasn't much of an obstacle for Abe, though. His girlfriend was dreamy and very sexy. She stayed for a spaghetti dinner but had to head home for her 8:00 curfew.

Now Abe and Gene took turns playing his guitar—Abe Spanish and Gene pop. Abe just loved the way Gene and I sang old rock songs. We really had to pick our brains to keep coming up with singable tunes that we knew the words to. We sat on his warm, starlit balcony eating ice cream and enjoying each other's music.

I really was shocked at how good life can be for some and how relatively miserable it can be for others. Hanging out with Abe was a very rosy picture of Tehran—which is not a very rosy city. I had never cared about, or even noticed, what I was now realizing was a big ethical issue: the giant difference between rich people and poor people. Not between rich and poor countries...but the difference within countries. Later on, we watched Iranian TV. Iran is so geared to the USA that they have an American TV channel and radio station designed to broadcast locally in English. Abe and his friends just love to sit around and watch such classics as *Rawhide, Top Cat,* and *Bob Newhart.* The strange thing is, there are no commercials! I never realized what a valuable function commercials fulfilled. I need a few minutes every now and then to rest, talk, or take a quick pee. Iranian TV is intense. It never lets up.

We watched the English news which seems to be more of a daily reminder that instability reigns all over this corner of the earth. You can't put a price tag on the value of being an American. Stability. I really wouldn't want it any other way. I am spoiled.

Abe, Gene, and I had a great discussion about politics and economics relative to distinct cultures. Abe's obviously in a very good spot in Iranian society. We talked about Iran's current turmoil—how the Western-backed dictator, the Shah, is being threatened by a simmering revolution. Abe supported the Shah, saying idealistic, anti-Shah college students are well-meaning, but they don't realize that most Iranians just couldn't handle all the freedoms that Americans have if they were just given to them overnight. According to Abe, the Shah did an experiment by giving Tabriz total freedom and, apparently, the people there nearly tore the city apart. The Shah had to step in and enforce his kind of order. But Abe was also realistic, and granted that it was very possible the Shah's days might be numbered.

Gene and I bedded down in Abe's living room...happy not to be back in Amir Kabir.

※　※　※

In Iran, the last Shah was still in power, but just barely. His portraits, which permeated society, seemed ready to crash to the ground.

No good tourist would leave Tehran
without seeing its trademark—
the Shah's Shahyad monument.

Gene was still feeling pretty rough—he had a fever and was quite down. We went to the pharmacy. For a minute it was thought that he might have cholera, which had recently broken out in Turkey. But Gene's shots were up to date. We gave him some pill to break the fever and then brought Gene back to Abe's. What an opportune time to have such a good local friend and a refuge where Gene can hopefully get better.

Still, I was worrying about him and wishing I could do something to help. I was also thinking how hard our trip ahead still was, and how hard it would be to have to restructure the trip if we turned back.

Then things rather quickly turned around. Somehow, we managed to get tickets on tomorrow's bus to Mashhad. We ran into our Spanish friends from the Istanbul-Tehran trip who were also going to Mashhad. That was a good feeling. Then we picked up our Afghanistan visas and celebrated back at Abe's with the last of Miko's great Bulgarian cake and a very good, clean, carton of cold homogenized and pasteurized chocolate milk. A yummy treat.

While Gene took it easy, I explored Tehran. Abe told us that the most expensive taxi fare in town was 50 rials. We had been paying 100 to 150 rials. That was the end of that. It's so nice to know the going rate. With that knowledge, I now taxied all over this huge, hot city.

I checked out the glittering vault of royal jewels in the basement of Iran's biggest bank, then rode to the outskirts of the city to see Tehran's trademark—the Shah's Shahyad monument.

It's so easy to get a taxi or even a private car to give you a ride. If you just point to the pavement in front of you, random cars will stop and let you hop in. Sometimes they charge. But if you make a friend by the end of the ride—like I did here—you generally ride for free.

I hopped out where the city meets the vast and arid countryside and there, shining white over well-watered green lawns and fountains, stood the monument—like a squashed or very stunted Eiffel

Tower. Underneath was a dull museum but with a great media show making Iran look much better than could ever be possible in real life. How awesome its mountains, how noble its cities, and how splendid the nearly deified Shah all were. Too hot and tired to climb to the top, I walked around, enjoying the monument, then ran through the sprinklers like a little kid.

I was back at Abe's by 7:00. Gene had slept most of the day and said he felt at least good enough to plan to leave in the morning. Several friends, including Abe's sister, dropped by. Even if living under a dictator, Abe's place seemed like the fun place to be. We watched a little more American TV. Again, I was impressed by how Iranians gobble up American culture. After everyone left, I diligently made myself stamp, address, and start writing about 25 "obligatories" (as I call postcards to special people in my life). Abe taught me some fancy backgammon strategies, beating me three times very quickly, then I packed for the morning.

We checked on Gene. He was napping in the living room and Abe asked him if he wanted a pizza. That seemed like a silly question to a guy who was really sick. But Gene said he was well enough to have an omelet. Then Abe ran out and picked us up Iranian pizzas. Wow, pizza. Tehran is a long way from Italy.

Today we joined the pilgrims bound for Mashhad. We were up at 5:00 and Gene felt better. We had cake and coffee and Abe drove us down to the bus station. Doing his best to entice us to return someday soon, Abe bid us goodbye, saying, "Americans just blast their heads off when they see the Iranian ski slopes!" Goodbye dear friend and giver of fun and comfort.

We met our Spanish friends and boarded the bus ready for the long day's ride to Mashhad.

At 6:00, we pulled out: about 40 Muslim pilgrims going to their holy place and us five tourists who were curious enough to sit on this bus all day. The first six hours went by quickly. The bus was quiet, friendly, and orderly. The driver was safe and steady, stopping only rarely, and the scenery was dramatic. We passed through a high, rugged mountain pass right next to the highest mountains in western Asia.

The Spaniards played the Rolling Stones on their tape recorder, we read, enjoyed the scenery, and I made friends with a gorgeous little Persian girl in front of me. I took some pictures of her that may be prize winners.

After 12:00, we came out of the mountains and into a hot, humid, sticky plain that just went on and on. The dust-caked, one-story towns all looked the same and served only to slow down traffic. The seats didn't recline and the plastic seat cover was quite yucky in the muggy heat. I felt like I had two knees in my kidneys but that's just

This bus ride came with a
wonderful little friend.

the way some jerk designed the seats. My knees hate to spend the long day pressed tightly up against the too-close next seat, but—having already survived the Pirate's bus—they do it with barely a whimper.

The time dragged on. We spent a lot of time looking at our map and proving to ourselves that we've gone a very long way and we're nearly there now. The former may be true, but not the latter.

At a dinner stop, Gene had a chelo kebab, and I finally ate my can of ravioli that I bought in Frankfurt and carried all the way here. This was the third Italian dinner in a row: spaghetti, pizza, and now— saving the best for last—my delicious ravioli…cold and out of a can.

The last two hours dragged terribly until Gene started teaching me how to pick out the chords to songs without the music. That particular musical skill is my weakness and I wish so much that it could be my strength.

Thankfully the bus, while slow, was very steady and we were happy just to make it to Mashhad in one day.

We got in at midnight and it soon became apparent that there was not a room in town to be had. This was a very special holy time, and every Muslim and his brother was here. People were camped out on the roadsides for miles.

After failing to find a park that the police would let us sleep in, a friendly guy came to our rescue and got us a cab to take us to the Mashhad campground.

This place was great—complete with showers, a swimming pool, and soft grass to sleep on. All the tents and rooms were taken but for 100 rials, there was plenty of grass to sleep on. Our Spanish friends—better prepared—set out their sleeping bags and tent while Gene and I (who had no tent or sleeping bags) put on our warmest clothes and slept on our ponchos.

✳　✳　✳

For 10:00 we were in Tabriz just in time to witness the armored riot squads ready themselves for student trouble. Iran is quite repressive & the students don't like that much. Torture & firing squads don't humor the young of a country.

We all hoped we wouldn't sleep in Tabriz and happily we said goodby to pock-faced half-wit, picked up a 2nd driver, and sped right on through to Tehran.

Now everyone's spirits picked up - this journey would be over in the morning. The spaniards sang and clapped La Bamba etc, the Russian did opera while the little smiley Iranian boy directed with a cigarette, the pirate washed his feet, sprayed everyone with de-smeller, made up his bed, told us to shut-up, and went to sleep. I waited for the night to slowly pass by - chasing sleep & checking my sluggish watch. I'm too tall for those chairs and my neck suffers when I hang myself to sleep. I tried everything but comfort eluded me. I did catch a few hours sleep between chai stops. Iran will be quite different. I can tell by the truck-stops. Quite cheap, dull food and crazy people.

When would this night end.

Monday July 24th   Teheran, Iran

Them long night ended with the long
bus ride. After four nights and three days
we had travelled from Istanbul to Teheran.
That's 2500 long kilometers (1500 miles). Only
4500 more kilometers (2700 miles) to go + we'll
be in Delhi!

My body from neck to tail ached but it
sure felt good to get off that Mihan Tour bus.
Teheran is huge (4,000,000 people) busy, sprawling,
and very hard for me to get oriented in.

We said goodby to our bus mates, took
a picture of the pirate and set off to take
care of business in Teheran.

Business consisted of changing money getting
an Afganistan visa, getting a bus ticket to
Meshad + finding a hotel - a lot of work.
Changing money was easy. We got $100 US cash
for emergencies + bribes that we anticipated
but hoped we wouldn't need on the road to
India. The visa was easy enough. We had to
leave our passports + 3 photos at the embassy
and pick them up tomorrow for $7. Now for
the problem we didn't anticipate. If there was
trouble we thought it would be getting into
Afganistan. The trouble was in getting to Meshad.
Wouldn't you know it - there is a big religous
festival in that most holy city and we couldn't
find any ride there for several days. The
busses were all booked solid, the train station was
chaos and we considered flying over it or
hitch hiking. Finally, as a half way measure,
we booked a bus to a town about 1/2 way

Iran

The warm sun nudged me awake. Our Spanish friends found that there was a bus to Afghanistan tomorrow, so we would spend the day in Mashhad.

This was a holy city at a holy time, and it was full of people trying to be holy at the holy shrine. The minute we left the campsite, we were hustled by salesmen preying on tourists. It was kind of strange. The campsite was for pilgrims and travelers only and local Iranians would gather around the fences and peer in. It was nice to have such a refuge.

Pointing to the pavement to get a ride Iranian-style worked great. In an instant, a guy pulled over. He drove us to buy our bus tickets, then he took us to the main sight in town—the shrine. But first, he invited us up for awful tea and his motives became clear: he wanted to sell us rugs and turquoise. We excused ourselves and made our way to the shrine.

The holy Imam Reza shrine was gorgeous with its turquoise dome gleaming in the hot blue sky. Pilgrims all flocked there and we were the only non-Muslims. We followed the pilgrim crowds and as we walked, there was always some guy following us telling us not to go closer and come to his shop. We worked our way right up to the elaborate gates and then could look in where Christians cannot go. We had an interesting time mingling and gawking.

After hosing each other down to cool off, we ventured into the bazaar. We shared a melon, checked out an old mosque, cleverly ditched a disturbingly friendly clinger, and walked down a long, quiet street.

We were starving and in search of food. Strangely, finding food was a formidable task in Mashhad. I bought a liter of milk which turned out to be something else in a milk carton. Then we stumbled into a bread shop and studied their interesting mass production of flat breads cooked as if slapping small pizza crusts onto the hot wall of an underground oven. It wasn't clear if this was wholesale or retail...but we managed to buy some.

56

Visiting the Mashhad Holy Shrine

Friendly Iranians gathered to see what was up with the vagabond Yankees who had just dropped in.

Iran

We were very hot and tired and Gene felt sick. That seems to be our condition a lot of the time lately. We caught a ride back to the campground and sacked out. We went for a refreshing swim, baked in the fierce sun, and wrote in our journals. We got a tent with a real bed tonight for 150 rials instead of 100 for a piece of the grass. Much better.

I sat by the pool writing and then went out to try and buy some dinner. Many things added up to really bring me down on this place. I wanted some French cheese but the guy in the store tried to charge me twice what he did the lady before me. So, I walked on through the filthy, dusty streets in my protective shell ignoring the faceless little "Hello Misters" and not finding anything but apples and milk that I knew were safe to eat.

Back in the campground, Gene and I got talking about diarrhea, which he had and I didn't. I shouldn't have said that because a few minutes later I heard it knocking and ran off to the toilet.

We went to the campground restaurant and shared the only meal we could stomach: a bowl of lemony soup with bread and our iodine-treated water. We have passed a kind of boundary: the end of safe water. From now on it's iodine or halazone tablets. We must have looked funny—two grown men sharing a meager bowl of soup. And it didn't even hit the spot.

But we were looking forward to tomorrow—on to Afghanistan. Knowing we had to be up at 6:00 without any alarm clock, we headed back to our tent. I ushered out a giant green grasshopper type bug and we slept fine.

not finding anything but apples and milk that was fit to eat.

Back in the campground Gene & I were talking about diarrhea which he had & I didn't. I commented that I had had no problems in 8 weeks of travel this summer. I shouldn't have said [...] because about 5 minutes [...] it knocking & ran off

We went up to the bowl of lemony soap w[...] treated water. We ha[...] safe water & from no[...] h[...] we [...]

Saturday, July 29   Meshad - Herat

My Spanish friend woke me at 5:45. I think
I would have slept all morning if he hadn't
have come in. We caught a ride down to
the station and, weakly, I searched for
breakfast. Half a liter of milk & a small cake
did quite a *[obscured]* and we were on our way.

Here *[obscured]*
Afghanis *[obscured]*
Iranians + *[obscured]*
bus station *[obscured]*
was prett *[obscured]*
most we *[obscured]*
bus, *[obscured]*
[obscured]
sa *[obscured]*

Afghanistan

July 29
August 4

Afghanistan, here we come!

Our bus sped east from Mashhad. Filled mostly with Afghans, we got a taste of a new world before we even reached its border. They look more Asian or Mongolian compared to Iranians, especially with their twine-wrapped bundles of belongings.

Gene and I were quiet and weak. I just sat there at the open window—not moving or talking, hot wind blowing in my face with my hair whipping around, hoping the kilometers would tick by, and knowing I was plunging farther and farther away from Europe.

At 10:30 we came to the Iran-Afghanistan border. What a place! Just stuck in the middle of nowhere.

An exhibit filling dusty glass cases with a stern message greeted us. It told the stories of many ill-fated drug smugglers—who tried to smuggle what in, how they were caught, and where they are doing time in prison. I have this terrible fear that someone will plant some dope in my rucksack and I'll get framed. That would be no fun at all.

We breezed through Iranian customs, but as it turned out, this would be just the first hurdle of the day. Next, we walked across a windy desert no man's land to the Afghan customs.

We just stood there. It was a desolate place bordered by abandoned, disassembled VW vans. A crowd of local people waited, piling into small orange buses as they arrived one at a time to shuttle them onward. The wind and heat were fierce. The barren plain stretched out in every direction. I turned to Gene and said: "So this is Afghanistan."

Afghanistan

We found shade in one of the wrecked VW vans and peeled a small apple. Then a bus came and we piled in. Stopping for a quick passport check, I couldn't believe it was so easy. It wasn't.

A few minutes later our bus pulled into the customs search yard, and we unloaded to sit and wait for the bank and doctor's office to open up.

And here I sit. The time is good for catching up in the journal, which I finally did. (It occurs to me how, when you're right up to date, journal writing can be more vivid...how you can do a better job.) As I flick and brush big ants off me and shield my eyes from sand and blowing things, I fantasize about all the fun things I could be doing. I think of friends back home in Seattle, of my parents on their boat in the cool, green San Juan Islands, and the fun I could be having in Europe. I'm glad I'm finally doing this but I'm really looking forward to the end of it all. I'm hoping for health, minimal hassles, and finding a good flight home.

The next few hours of Afghan customs tried our patience. First, the funny little bank opened up. To change my 100-franc note I had to make three signatures, write down the serial number of the bill, and ask several times until I got the correct change. Next we bounced from one dusty office to the next getting all the red tape taken care of so we could enter Afghanistan.

They stopped Gene—it turns out he was missing a shot on his yellow International Certificate of Vaccination, which we show at each border. We were sent to a little clinic. There we waited and waited some more. The doctor finally dropped by to give Gene his shot. I will never forget the sight of his dull needle bending as he forced it into Gene's arm.

We shuffled to the next gauntlet. The luggage "search" was little more than a glance, our shot certificates were checked again, and the police and the customs officers checked us out, so we were done—or so we thought. About 100 yards later there was yet another police

The Iran-Afghanistan border was a godforsaken place where customs officials, police, and con artists seemed to outnumber travelers. From there, we negotiated a bus ride to the first city in Afghanistan, Herat.

Rest stop entertainment?
A goat being skinned.

check—which the Polish travelers flunked, so we all had to wait while they went through more red tape. Finally, after five long hours at the border, we were cleared, and could now enter Afghanistan.

❋   ❋   ❋

Back on another orange bus, we were on our way, heading into the dusty vastness of arid Afghanistan. The countryside was dry and barren, backed by stark brown mountains, and broken every once in a while by a cluster of mud huts, some old ruins, or a herd of goats or sheep. It always feels good to enter a new country. Everything that lies ahead is as new as can be.

Just when we were finally getting somewhere, a dispute broke out in the front of the bus. We learned that the Afghans had just decided to double the price of the ride from 50 to 100 afghanis. That's only pennies to us, so why not? But we tourists were stubborn. We talked among ourselves and collectively decided to refuse.

The driver turned the bus around and started to take us back to the Iranian border unless we paid. One rugged looking Afghan pulled a knife. A big knife. You could say they had us over a barrel.

There was an uproar as everyone was trying to solve the problem at once. One soft-spoken but commanding Pakistani convinced us to pay 60 afghanis—so the driver turned the bus back around. The conductor came to collect, but we all feared if we paid there was nothing stopping them from pulling the same trick again. So we compromised—giving them 30 afghanis now and promising the rest upon arrival. After that episode we were all on edge, and I think if they tried to get any more money, they would have had a riot from their now-worldly bus load of hardened travelers.

We stopped at a rest stop that gave Gene and me our first good look at Afghanistan. It was a barren place: a ramshackle tea house, a well, and a rickety sign reading "hotel." Gene and I just stood there watching a bunch of locals skinning a still-warm goat. At least the leaky well provided everyone with cold, filthy water. I wallowed in it, really cooling down nicely. We shared a 25-cent melon and my weak, starving body gobbled it down.

The tea house was exactly the image I had of an Afghanistan tea house. I stood over my melon rinds looking in the window like I was watching a documentary on TV. Old, traditionally clad men, who looked like they worked hard but who never seem to do anything but lazily sit around, were cross-legged on threadbare rugs on the floor drinking tea and smoking hashish. The room filled with smoke and their glassy dark eyes seemed to smile. What a bizarre society. I guess when materially you're so far behind you just give up—sit in the shade eating melons, drinking tea, and smoking hash. Then the word spread—our driver was high, too, and the crew would be quite mellowed out.

We all climbed back on the hot bus and headed to our final destination—the town of Herat. As we bumped along, feeling as rugged as the countryside, Gene and I decided that from now on we'd raise our standard of living. I've really abused myself. For two days I've basically lived on pop and melons. We vowed that, for our mental and physical health and to keep our spirits high, going forward, we'd eat well and stay in good hotels.

What did the people think as we
waltzed in and out of their lives?

Afghanistan towns invited exploration.

Pulling into Herat, our Hippie Trail kicked into high gear. Right away it dawned on us: "You know, this place looks quite nice." Very green as far as towns in this part of the world go and with lots of parks. Herat was, like our minimal guidebook said, "hard not to like."

Sick of cheap, scuzzy holes, I lobbied for a first-class hotel. We found a dilly. Hotel Mowafaq, the fanciest hotel in downtown Herat ($5), was just what we needed: centrally located, showers, swimming pool, clean restaurant, and free of con men and hustlers. There's air conditioning in the hall, and a bug screen on our open window. Rather than dangling homeless, the light has a fixture. I feel like a softy, but here I can leave my stuff without worrying, walk around in bare feet without picking up a fungus, and get easy peace when I need it.

I enjoyed a lovely cold shower and a successful stint on the real sit-down toilet. You don't appreciate life's little things until you don't have them. Downstairs we ordered soup, bread, rice, meat, and cold water for 50 afghanis ($1.25). We were both thirsty, and the cold water attacked our self-discipline like forbidden fruit. Was it safe? We succumbed to it and it sure tasted good. Black and green tea in good sized pots finished the meal nicely and I can't believe how everything about this trip has turned around so wonderfully.

With a full stomach and fluffy hair, we headed out into the Herat evening. We had a Sprite and walked around the central square.

We were definitely in a new and different culture, and both Gene and I perked up. The people here are welcoming, and police are present on the streets keeping order. Horse-drawn, chariot-like, flower-decorated taxis charged down the streets, bells jingling. Afghanistan.

We stopped into a small clothing shop to check out some local clothes to go "native" for the rest of the trip. We didn't get any now, but we both decided that baggy clothes make a lot more sense in the heat and would make us stick out less.

Gene did buy one thing from the guy in the shop—a small chunk of hashish.

Hashish. Hash. Pure cannabis resin. So that's what it looks like.

Getting high for my first time has been on my list of desired experiences for this trip, so...We'll see.

We headed back to the hotel, to go to bed early and get a fresh start on tomorrow. We stood on our breezy balcony, overlooking this exotic-looking city, thinking there's no place on earth we'd rather be. On the street it seems everything's so different. Yet the constellations overhead felt like old friends. We both agreed that it's so important to live well and enjoy oneself. And, without going through periods of misery and discomfort, you can't really know what it is to enjoy. With this trip, I'm getting better at enjoyment. I'm becoming more appreciative.

I punched Gene on the shoulder and said, "Ok, now our trip begins!"

✻　✻　✻

After a hearty breakfast of fried eggs, yogurt, and a pot of black chai, I cleaned my camera lenses, and Gene and I set out to see Herat.

First stop: change money. The ragtag bank was a sight in itself. Waiting my turn, I saw tattered Afghans lugging in big suitcases, and a uniformed guard with a bayonet long enough to skewer two

No museums, no turnstiles. Just stroll down the street, immersed in Afghanistan at work and at play. Every few meters, there was another shop with a hard-working businessman.

*Many vehicles in Afghanistan
are still horse-drawn.*

or three bank robbers at once. Mysterious tribesmen came in with American $100 bills—I'm afraid to imagine where they got them.

It took forever to change my $100. I was supposed to have 3,858 afghanis coming to me. First the guy gave me 3,000. I said "more." He gave me 800. "More," I said, and got 50 more. Finally I asked for—and got—the last 8 afghanis.

Tucking in my money belt, we stepped outside. Now we were free to ramble.

I had a Fanta, put on my zoom lens, and went into action. We ventured down a dreamy side street full of colorful, flowery, horse-drawn taxis, busy craftsmen, fruit stands, and dust. Each man who passed looked like something straight out of a hundred-year-old travel poster. Strong powerful eyes behind leathery weather-beaten faces. Poetic wind-blown beards long and scraggily and turbans like snakes wrapping protectively around their heads.

We wandered away from the center to a dusty residential area churning with activity. I studied people's reactions to us. I didn't really know how they accepted us strange short-panted, pale-skinned, weak-stomached, finnicky people who came into their world to gawk, take pictures, and buy junk to bring home and tell everyone how cheap it was—not a flattering contrast with these hardy, proud people who work so hard and live so simply.

By now, the afternoon temperature was cooking, and we soaked our heads under a faucet. We worked up a mean thirst and shared a watermelon in the shade. After mailing a few postcards (will they ever even get home?), we checked out a row of cloth weavers. Hard-working men ran these ingeniously primitive looms tirelessly.

We found ourselves in a neighborhood of very hard-sell shops. Like running the gauntlet, we made our way in and out of shops. I dove right into the local custom of bargaining hard, and found I was really getting into it. I bought an exciting fox hat and three nicely embroidered pouches. I haven't bought any souvenirs in two months of travel—and now I'm afraid I've opened the floodgates.

One pseudo-friendly guy took me by the hand and physically walked me into his shop and before I knew it, I was wearing the wonderful white baggy pants and shirt and turban of the local people. I was determined to work him down from 500 afghanis to my ceiling of 150. He claimed to be incredibly insulted—why the cloth alone was worth 200! I was getting tired of always wearing my shorts and yellow t-shirt. I went on a bit of a spree and soon had a whole new outfit—baggy, lightweight drawstring pants, a white "work shirt," and two handwoven wool vests. I was happy with my new outfit. I just wonder if I'll like it back in Seattle.

Next, I tried for a lovely mink pelt, that caught my eye. Twice I threatened to walk away if he didn't give me my price. We went back and forth, back and forth, and I was almost there. But suddenly he surprised me—no deal!—and just let me walk away empty handed. This guy is good. He knows I really want that mink! Maybe, if I can swallow my pride, I'll go back tomorrow and haggle on.

By now Gene and I were exhausted, so we headed back to our lovely hotel for a cold shower and a bite to eat. Then we wet down our sheets for added coolness and took a short nap. We have money in our pockets and it feels so good to just spend it when you want and not worry. We both agreed: after weeks of hard travel, we're really living well.

Ready to take "going local" to new heights, I stopped by a tailor in Herat, got measured, and purchased a made-to-order, all-white outfit.

One tooth still makes a big smile in Herat, Afghanistan.

Gene pulled out his hunk of hash and set it on the bed. Then and there I decided—this would be the time and place that I'd lose my "marijuana virginity." I've never even smoked a cigarette, and smoking pot has always turned me off, so to speak, because it's always an object of social pressure. I never felt comfortable doing it just because everyone at a party was doing it and I was the only "square" one. That kind of pressure and the usual scene surrounding pot smoking had always reinforced my determination to stay away from the evil weed.

But being here in Afghanistan, this made things different. In Afghanistan, hashish is an integral part of the culture. It's as innocent as wine with dinner is in America.

All along our trip, Gene and I have talked about marijuana. Gene had smoked it back home, so maybe it's not so awful. I decided that, if I felt good about the whole situation, I'd like to smoke some hash in Afghanistan. Well, here I am. I feel great, and I love this town. Here we go.

Gene had bought about half a domino worth of pure hashish for 40 afghanis ($1). It was so smooth as he sliced it with a knife. Now he mixed it with some tobacco and piled it into a funny, old, straight wood pipe we picked up. He took a drag—immediately remarking, "Good stuff."

I sucked in, not knowing what to expect and hoping not to get a mouth full of ashes. I don't like smoke, but besides that, there was nothing repulsive about it. It didn't even smell dank like marijuana.

The only problem was—nothing happened. I had smoked enough, but they say virgin runs are often unproductive. It felt good anyway—I had done it.

We had a light dinner, then went back to our room to smoke a bit more. This time I sensed a bit of a change. Certain colors were more tangy. Things had a vibrant edge that I didn't realize was an option. I was very relaxed, and the light fixture on our ceiling looked like a big candle breathing in and out. I lay there wondering how cockroaches got their name. But I still wasn't really high.

Or, maybe I was…

I went out on the hotel balcony to tell the old cleaning man we needed more toilet paper. "Look," he said dreamily, "isn't it beautiful?" We both stood motionless watching as the sun sank behind the distant mountain. I guess people all over the world enjoy the same things.

Gene and I went downstairs, where a big wedding was just getting started. The bride's father proudly shook my hand and welcomed us in. We didn't crash the party, it crashed us. Everyone was dressed quite formal. The men were in one room singing, the women in the other dancing, while the decorated car waited parked outside. We sat next to the little Afghan band listening to the exciting music and watching the women dance. It was clear that we were being treated to the equivalent of Herat's night at the opera.

When things started to wind down, we took a nighttime walk, ready to mingle. Mingling was a bit intensified. I didn't know if it was because of the hashish or because I was in a very good mood. I was tickled by little things, like a man weighing tomatoes. Hustlers became playful. I was more receptive to would-be pests…ready to poke around a little more freely.

The sun had gone down, and lanterns came on. Chariots with torches charged through the darkness, and men passed by swinging fiery lanterns. Herat is small but it really doesn't matter because no street is ever the same if you walk through it a second or third time.

We went from shop to shop very casually, nosing in, and just poking around. Shopkeepers and the work boys squatted around soup and bread. Many Afghans were high or getting there. Old women totally covered by bag-like outfits carried children and called out, strangely enough, for photos. The evening was cool, and the wind howled.

The night was a great experience and we kept wandering. Gene and I shared a small melon. A strange dog knocked my glasses off my bag and the lens fell out. I panicked but—thank goodness—it popped right back in, good as new.

I really got into some exciting photography. Existing light mixed with lantern light. I talked men into posing precisely how I wanted them, moving their chin up a tad or the lantern closer. However the pictures turn out, both my subject and I had a memorable time.

Countless moments and scenes like these blazed forever in my mind—a picture of Afghanistan.

It was getting late, so we started back to the hotel. But where were we? No problem: we flagged down a fancy two-wheeled, horse-drawn buggy taxi. Charging all over town as if in a torchlit chariot, Gene and I sang songs—really entertaining, or at least amusing, our driver. We laughed about what a great day today had been, and how much we were looking forward to tomorrow.

When we reached the hotel and hopped off, I surprised our driver by confidently paying him 10 afghanis, and he barely had time to gripe. These tourists weren't gonna be taken for a ride except on a horse! After three weeks on the road, we'd learned the trick: Don't agree to a price beforehand, or they'll know you're new at the game and rip you off. Just decide on a reasonable price, get on with confidence, sit back, and tell the driver—"Home James!"

✳ ✳ ✳

We picked up rental bikes in search of a little more adventure. It felt good to have wheels. We could take in more, we could stop when we wanted, the breeze cooled us off and, if things got too intense, we could make a clean escape.

Coasting happily down the road, we were surrounded by Herat: guys tossing melons, colorful girls sitting on curbs, lazy teenagers slouching on warm wagons, snippets of Afghan life.

The people here are genuinely friendly and proud, shaking my hand firmly and as equals. While I did get one small fruit thrown at me, all in all, this is one of the friendliest countries I've experienced. Of course, it's a different world for women. Any woman (and post-pubescent girl) who ventures onto the streets is totally covered up, seeing a man's world only through a tiny gridwork in the cloth that covers her face.

We headed for some old, ruined minarets in the distance. An old man let us into the historic mosque for 10 afghanis and we saw the tomb of an old Afghan king. Nearby, we stopped to chat with some studious types sitting in the shade. They told us about their culture and language—and also that we were spending too much money for everything! One guy asked, "Aren't you traveling with your women?" I told him my girlfriend is at home, and he replied, "Oh that must be very difficult for you—I could never do that." It made me think of home and my girlfriend, and—yes—I do feel like I've been "on the road" for a long time now.

We continued on, determined to pedal in one direction until we reached the edge of town. We made our way down the dusty street until the busy city became a mud village. We found ourselves enveloped in a new and different world. Quiet, brown mud streets were lined with high walls long and narrow, broken occasionally by small shops and rustic wooden doors. Young and old sat around as if they were waiting for a stranger on a bike to happen by.

I'm sure we were a very rare sight for them. I wondered if they enjoyed our presence or if we were violating their peace. I experimented with different greetings, from a stern military salute to a child's wave. I found that the solemn "kiss the hand and put it to the

*Trucks were exuberantly painted,
though many vehicles in Afghanistan
are still horse-drawn.*

I felt like we were bringing smiles
from distant lands to children
who were confused, curious,
and happy to see us.

heart"—that religious-looking Afghans offer us—gets great results.

Groups of kids constantly came up to us shouting "Hello, *baksheesh!*"—asking us for a gift. I'd brought a pocket full of candies that I feel better about giving than money.

We stopped off at a farm. A pile of hay was being romantically thrashed by a man driving a couple of oxen pulling a wooden hay-chewing device. What an opportunity! I pounced on the chance, gesturing to the man if I could drive the cart. Soon there I was, sitting on the chewer, driving the oxen around and around. I think the peasants got as big of a kick out of me as I got out of them and their hay.

As we pedaled back home for a cool-down, Gene and I reflected on what we'd seen. We agreed that people in this happy society seem surprisingly content. I've seen no hunger and very few hard-case beggars. They have modest needs for their meager productivity and things seem to work out just fine. And there's more than enough tea, hashish, and melons for everyone.

We returned our bikes, picked up a melon, and retreated to our hotel. Feeling hot but happy, we stripped to our underwear and took a chilly plunge in the pool. Instant refreshment! Wow! We frolicked around, took a few dives, relaxed in the sun and I thought, "My goodness—this is what a vacation is supposed to be."

Dripping up to the room, Gene and I agreed: for the rest of this trip, "good sleep, good food, and a good hotel" would be our winning formula.

The sun was lower in the sky by the time we stepped back out into Herat.

We ran into a guy we'd met on the Istanbul-Tehran bus, who recommended we check out Herat's "endless bazaar." He was right. With every step, the bazaar brought something new, sometimes things we couldn't even understand. Each shop was five yards across, so every five yards was a new scene—a new window into Afghan life. What a sensual experience!

We morphed or melted from scene to scene soaking in all the "bazaar" images. I put my zoom lens on and got such a thrill out of zooming in on these lovely people. I can hardly wait to see how my pictures turned out, but it'll have to be after we get home—there's no place to develop them on the road.

The workers were fascinating. We'd pass from water-pipe-making souks, to tin pounders, weavers, beadmakers, bead stringers, people working bellows, people sharpening knives on rickety foot-powered wheels, chain pounders, and nail benders. Everything was hand-done. Old and young worked furiously at the same menial task all day long, all life long. I'll never again complain about a long day of my work teaching piano lessons.

By now we were exhausted, and we needed to pack for our bus ride across Afghanistan in the morning.

But first, I had one last crucial bit of business. We stopped by to check out my old friend—the mink pelt. This was my third time in the guy's shop and I knew if I went home without that mink, I'd kick myself. I was soon bargaining furiously again. Gene helped out by pretending to be bored and wanting to leave. It took forever, but I finally got the guy down to 460 afghanis ($12) and came away with a great skin. I love it, just like I loved that old stray cat I befriended and brought home in second grade who ended up giving me ring-worm. So that's what I named my new mink—"Ringworm."

Gene and I hopped in a funny little three-wheeled taxi that looked like a souped-up ice cream truck. Back at the hotel, where the waiters all know us, we dug into a hearty, meaty meal topped with tea and a melon. I feel so good. We've been drinking the water and haven't gotten sick. I feel in control, and anything I desire, I can just get. Wow. We are living so fantastically. Up in the room, I took a long shower, cleaned up my pack for tomorrow, and hit the sack, ready for the next step in our journey.

The Qaderi bus from Herat to Kabul

*On a long bus ride, this mom
and daughter stared at me, and
I pondered the lot of women in
this male-dominated world.*

Our **"express bus"** to **Kabul** left **very early.** Dawn was cracking as we stepped along sidewalks lined with sleeping people. In the distance, we could hear our boisterous bus honking loudly as if it was psyching itself up for the 800-kilometer ride that lay ahead. We were wondering exactly what "express" would mean.

The bus was organized and punctual, and we were soon moving at a steady pace, following a solitary electricity line that accompanied the narrow, but well-paved, US- and USSR-built road across the Afghanistan desert.

The countryside was desolate, hot, and foreboding. A herd of camels, a stray nomad or cluster of quiet tents, a mud-brick ruin melting like a sandcastle after being hit by a wave.

For our first bathroom break, the driver just pulled the bus over in the middle of the desert. The men peed on one side of the road. The women, gathering on the other side, turned their black robes into one-person tents, and squatted with wrap-a-round privacy. Seeing a dozen short, round, black-clad figures dotting the hard pan ground reminded me of some strange chess game or a game of "whirling dervish statue-maker."

We also made three punctual stops to pray to Mecca. Everyone got out, kneeled, and bowed in the same direction. As the only ones not partaking, we felt awkward.

Then we were off again—the same barren landscape, the same lazy, goofy camels, the same sleepy gray-brown mud-brick castle towns, and stark dirt mountains making a jaggy skyline. I wrote a poem called "Afghan Eyes" about a little girl who stared at me for five straight hours.

Darkness was falling as we approached Kabul. Gene wasn't feeling well. Our bus was flagged down and soldiers got on—looking for guns, I assume. The word on the bus was that Afghanistan was undergoing political upheaval—a "People's Revolution," instigated by the Soviet Union. I hope it doesn't affect our trip.

Finally, 14 hours later, we entered Kabul. We took a cab to touristy "Chicken Street" and found the nicest hotel we could—the not-too-nice, but ok, Sina Hotel. Gene went straight to bed—I'm worried about him. I can only hope he's better—and I'm still good—in the morning. I had a so-so dinner at our so-so hotel.

Oh well, at least I'm in Kabul. Imagine that. So close to my dream: the Khyber Pass and India. Though I'll have to check a globe to be sure, I definitely feel like I'm halfway around the world from home.

❊ ❊ ❊

It's sinking in—Gene's really sick. It could be dysentery. There was a German girl at the hotel who also had "Tehran tummy" and she told me she just wanted to go home. Home is a very nice thought anytime you're on the road to India. It's even more appealing when you're sick.

Our friendly hotel owner promised, by Allah, to take care of Gene with his magic "sick man's tea." Until he's better, we can't move on. I suddenly have time to kill.

It was already hot by the time I set out alone into Kabul. I had no map or information. I really couldn't get oriented in this blobby, hodgepodge capital. The city is like a giant village sprawling out along several valleys. Where those valleys came together was downtown. Kabul seems to love its sadly dried-up river, which has very

Kabul, Afghanistan

little water with a wide and rocky bed. It was hot and dusty, and shade was rare.

I walked down "Chicken Street," the touristic high-pressure point of Afghanistan, expertly ignoring the countless "Come into my shop mister" invitations and realizing that out of all the junk everyone's trying to sell, there was nothing I really wanted.

Next, I checked on bus tickets to Pakistan. Then, with several incredibly persistent "shoeshine" beggar boys chasing after me, I ducked into the Pakistani embassy to confirm that Americans need no visas. (Thank goodness.) Then I continued on through chaotic Kabul.

Evidence of the recent "People's Revolution" is everywhere. There's an 11:00 curfew, propaganda posters, and soldiers are everywhere with poised bayonets. I saw what was left of a tank, blown to bits and left as a reminder that the old regime was dead. Though I don't really understand the situation, the USSR seems hell-bent on getting messed up in Afghanistan and my hunch is that they're underestimating the spine of this poverty-stricken nation.

I caught a taxi to the Kabul Museum. It was a long ride and the driver fiercely demanded 60 afghanis. I thought 40 was very fair, but finally just to lose him, I paid 50—only to find that the museum was closed anyway. A horde of little children crowded around me and wouldn't give up asking for "baksheesh," and I had to duck into a mosque where a policeman chased them away.

It seemed like everyone was hassling me, so I hopped onto a crowded bus and rode it to its end. I ended up just where I wanted to be—generic, neighborhood Kabul. It had a number of large fancy buildings, but the tribal chaos still permeated everything—old men with donkey loads of tomatoes, little girls selling limes, piles of honeydew melons with a guy sitting on top sleepily smoking hash.

I felt very obvious being white, alone, and wearing shorts. Being so rich (even as a lowly backpacker) and so white in this poor and struggling corner of our world puts me in a strange bind as a traveler.

It's sad, but I realized today that I tend to build a wall between me and any potential friends. In Europe, I love to talk with people and make friends—that's a big reason I travel. But here there's something in the way. I think a lot of it is suspicion, lack of understanding, and fatigue. Also, most of the people here who do speak English, seem to speak it only to make money off the tourist. I wish I could totally trust people. And I wish I spoke the local language. But I can't and I don't.

I was hungry, so I escaped into the "Afghan Store," the closest thing to a Western department store, and found a nice restaurant with a beautiful view of ugly Kabul.

An old man had me sit with him. "I am professor so and so," he said, and then asked, "What is your name and fame?" He was very excited to have a meal with an American and practice his English. I wasn't in the mood, but I taught him the do-re-me scale and what a "radish" was—the only thing on my plate that stumped him in English. I'm afraid I wasn't very friendly, but he said he would never forget his meal with "Mr. Rick."

Before he left, he told me, "A third of the people on this planet eat with spoons and forks like you, a third of the people eat with chopsticks, and a third of the people eat with their fingers like me... and we're all civilized just the same."

As I headed home, I thought: That professor was right. I had thought less of people like him who ate with their fingers. And I was wrong—ethnocentric. I was thankful for the lesson he taught me... that "we're all civilized just the same."

※　※　※

Back at the hotel Gene was sitting up in the courtyard, drinking his "sick man's tea" and reading the last half of the memoir of Nikita Khrushchev. (We had ripped it in two so we could both read it on the same bus ride.)

In Kabul, Afghanistan

Hoping to blend in better, I changed into a pair of Gene's baggy, white Afghan pants. I grabbed my camera and caught a bus to the edge of town. It's kind of nice not knowing or caring where you're going. I just boarded any old bus, paid one afghani, and rode it for as long as I wanted—which was the end of the line. When we got there, the bus driver invited me to a nearby café for tea. I accepted, and soon there was a whole gang gathered around us—to stare. Boy, I must really be a strange-looking dude to these people.

On the way home, I dropped by the "American Center" and was surprised to find Gene there, too—his first foray out in what seems like forever. We just relaxed and read their collection of *Time* magazines. The "people's" government had cut out any articles about the USSR, but even reading old and censored news was better than nothing. When you're on the road, getting a chance to immerse yourself in an American magazine or movie for a little while…it brings you home.

Gene finally had an appetite, and it was our last night in Afghanistan, so we decided to splurge on dinner. First, we made a point of changing all our old Iranian and Turkish money for Pakistani rupees. Everyone had warned us that clue-less backpackers changing money can be tricked into accepting old versions of a currency that's been taken out of circulation and is now worthless. We were always nervous we could be ripped off that way. Folding away our newly-purchased Pakistani rupees, we'll find out tomorrow if we have the right vintage.

Now we were determined to spend all our last afghanis before we hit Pakistan. So we chose the fancy "Steak House," where we got a very good steak-and-vegetable dinner (for a dollar) that hit our spots wonderfully.

Back at the hotel, I spent the evening in the courtyard repairing a strap on my pack and catching up in this journal, while enjoying tea and a Fleetwood Mac tape. Gene said it would be very good to be on the move again. I whispered, "Go East young man."

Friday, Aug 4th   Kabul - Rawalpindi, Pakistan

This was the morning I was psyched for. I don't think I could have woken up feeling bad and I didn't. Both Gene & I felt good. We had a last big Sina Hotel breakfast and caught our little 8:30 Pakistan bus.

This bus was the way I wanted to do Khyber Pass. I had dreamed of crossing this romantically wild & historically dangerous pass for years and it was very high on my life's checklist of things to do - in the top five for sure. Now I was sitting on this kinky old brightly but badly painted bus next to a wonderful open window that let me lean half of my body out if I wanted to. Our seats were big & high yet crowded and the bus was full of Pakistanis and the "Road to India" travellers.

I was glad to get out of Kabul and almost immediately we were in a scenic mountain pass. From here to the border, while nothing by Pacific Northwest standards was the closest thing to lush that we've seen in Afghanistan. We even crossed a lake - but I saw no boats. I wondered how many or how few Afgans had ever been in [...] leaving Jalalabad for a hurried [...]

Pakistan to India

August 4
August 6

Passports in hand we knew we were just
half-way through the process but we weren't sure
where to go next. We wandered into one ramshackle
building and in a dark room two men jumped up from
two cots & welcomed us to lay down. No thanks! We
got out of there & were overrun by dope dealers & black
market money changers. Everything was so open & blatant
that it almost seemed legal. We bought $10 worth of
Pakistan rupees & _____ our bags searched so
we'd be done frisking. In the chaos we just got on
the bus & skipped the baggage check. At our window
we were entertained by lots of hesh & a particularly
persistent man with a _____ bottle of cocaine — 4 grams
for $30. I took his _____ him to get lost.
Finally we were loaded & ready to do it — cross the
Khyber Pass. Boo I was thrilled to say the least. Physically,
it was just like any mountain pass but when you've
_____ & _____ about something for many
_____ special & this was an exciting time for
_____ Staring out the window I tried
_____ wild turn in the road every
_____ goat every gaily painted
_____ hut _____

Khyber Pass—where trucks rumble and backpackers celebrate a milestone on the Hippie Trail to Kathmandu.

Crossing the Khyber Pass has long been my dream. And this morning we'd do it. Our health was tenuous at best, but after three weeks on the road, both Gene and I were determined that nothing would stop us now. We swallowed our malaria pills with black tea and toast, and caught our 8:30 bus to Pakistan.

Now I was sitting on this kinky old brightly-but-badly painted bus next to a wonderful open window that let me lean half of my body out. Our seats were big and high and the bus was crowded—full of Pakistanis and "Hippie Trail" travelers. Except for a little smear of yesterday's vomit still dried to the outside of the bus below my window, this was exactly the way I wanted to do the Khyber Pass.

The Khyber Pass! I had dreamed of crossing this romantically wild and historically dangerous cultural divide for years. It was very high on my life's checklist of things to do—in the top five for sure. I'd read all about its illustrious history as the gateway to India. Now I was following in the footsteps of Genghis Khan, Alexander the Great, and countless Silk Road traders.

I was glad to get out of Kabul. Almost immediately we were in a scenic mountain landscape. While nothing by Pacific Northwest standards, it was the closest thing to lush that we've seen in Afghanistan. We even passed a lake, but I saw no boats. I wondered how many, or how few, Afghans had ever been in a boat.

After a hurried lunch break in Jalalabad, we were soon nearing the border, and apprehension grew. We hoped it wouldn't be too much of a hassle but by now nothing surprised us.

The Afghan side, while time consuming, was easy. We sat around eating a melon, waiting our turn to be searched. We filled out the form, got our passports stamped—the usual process—and loaded back on, only to stop 100 yards later for our introduction to Pakistan.

Pakistani customs was pretty unruly. We all piled into a room, and one by one were called up to the desk while the customs official "hunt and pecked" our vital statistics into his register and stamped our passports.

Passports in hand, we weren't sure where to go next. We wandered into a ramshackle building. There, in a dark room, two men jumped up from two cots and welcomed us to lie down. No thanks! We got out of there.

Next we were overrun by black-market money-changers. Everything was so open and blatant that it almost seemed legal, so we bought $10 worth of Pakistan rupees. Finally, frustrated by the chaos, we just skipped the baggage check and got back on the bus. At our window we were entertained by a horde of dope dealers: lots of hash sellers and a particularly persistent man with a small bottle of cocaine—4 grams for $30. I snuck a photograph and told him to get lost.

Finally, we were loaded and ready to do it—to cross the Khyber Pass. I was thrilled. Physically, it was just like any other rocky mountain pass, but when you've wondered, dreamed, and thought about something for many years, it becomes special…it gains a mystique.

Up and up the bus climbed. Hanging out the window, I tried to take in everything—every wild turn in the road, every fortress-crowned hill, every stray goat, every gaily painted truck that passed us, and every mud hut. Flags flying from fortresses of stacked rocks

*Leaving Afghanistan on the
Khyber Pass, we passed through
Waziristan, long a virtually
ungovernable "autonomous region"
where Pashtun tribes made their own
rules and handled their own defense.*

In Peshawar, the leading Pashtun city, people walked around with rifles slung over their shoulders.

were as tattered as the men behind those rocks. Were they guarding something…or hiding out? I wish I knew. One thing was clear: they seemed fiercely independent and well beyond the reach of any modern government.

We stopped in a tribal village to pay a toll for the privilege of passing through (safely). I looked at the rugged people—the Pashtun tribesmen who've controlled this strategic chokepoint for centuries. The men stood around with rifles ignoring the bus and gathered in circles trading both goods and stories…or perhaps conspiring. As I saw the people who inhabited this treacherous pass, I wondered who they were, how they lived, what stories could they tell.

Emerging from the Khyber Pass we started our descent into Pakistan. Dry, stony graveyards with wind-tattered flags littered the hillsides. Except for the flags, there was no color—just dirt and rocks. Clouds threatened. We were moving out of the arid Arab side of South Asia and into the wet Indian subcontinent. From now on we would feel muggy—but enjoy the green countryside. In just a few minutes we were in Peshawar. Today is a good day—lots of miles covered, a new country, and I had crossed the Khyber Pass.

Friday, Aug 4th   Kabul ~ Rawalpindi, Pakistan

This was the morning I was psyched for. I
don't think I could have woken up feeling bad
and I didn't. Both Gene & I felt good. We
had a last big Sina Hotel breakfast and caught
our little 8:30 Pakistan bus.

This bus was the way I wanted to do Khyber
Pass. I had dreamed of crossing this romantically
wild & historically dangerous pass for years and
it was very high on my life's checklist of things
to do - in the top five for sure. Now I was
sitting on this kinky old brightly but badly
painted bus next to a wonderful open window
that let me lean half of my body out if I
wanted to. Our seats were big & high yet
crowded and the bus was full of Pakistanis
and the "Road to India" travellers.

I was glad to get out of Kabul and almost
immediately we were in a scenic mountain pass.
From here to the border, while nothing by Pacific
Northwest standards was the closest thing to lush
that we've seen in Afganistan. We even passed a
lake - but I saw no boats. I wondered how many -
or how few - Afgans had ever been in a boat.

Stopping in Jalalabad for a hurried lunch break and
we were back on the road in 20 minutes. We were
nearing the boarder & apprehension grew. We hoped it
wouldn't be too much of a hassle but by now nothing
suprised us.

The Afganistan border station, while time consuming
was easy. We just sat around eating a mellon & wishing
we had money for a coke. Actually we had planned
our cash reserves very nicely & were leaving with no
Afganis. We waited our turn to be searched, filled
out the form got our passports stamped - the usual
process and loaded back on only to stop 100 yards
later for our introduction to Pakistan.

This place was pretty unruly. We piled into a
room & one by one we were called up to the
desk & the customs official "hunt & pecked"
our vital statistics into his register & stamped
our passports.

Passports in hand we new we were just half-way through the process but we weren't sure where to go next. We wandered into one ramshackle building and in a dark room two men jumped up from two cots & welcomed us to lay down. No thanks! We got out of there & were over-run by dope dealers & black market money changers. Everything was so open & blatant that it almost seemed legal. We bought $10 worth of Pakistan rupees & then tried to get our bags searched so we'd be done. Frustrated in the chaos we just got on the bus & skipped the baggage check. At our window we were entertained by lots of hash & a particularly persistent man with a small bottle of cocaine — 4 grams for $30. I took his picture & told him to get lost.

Finally we were loaded & ready to do it - cross the Khyber Pass. Ooo I was thrilled to say the least. Physically, it was just like any other rocky mountain pass but when you've wondered, dreamed & thought about something for many years it becomes special & this was an exciting time for me. Up the bus climbed. Hanging out the window I tried to take in everything — every wild turn in the road every fortress-crowned hill, every stray goat, every gaily painted truck that passed us and every mud hut. I looked at the rugged people who inhabited this treacherous pass & wondered who they were, how they lived, what stories could they tell. Dry rocky graveyards with wind tattered flags littered the hill sides. Clouds threatened. We were moving out of the Arab side of South Asia and into the wet Indian sub-continent. From now on we would feel muggy — but enjoy the green countryside.

We crossed the Khyber Pass and passed through a tribal village to pay a toll for the privilege. I could see the men armed with rifles ignoring the bus and gathered in circles trading good & stories.

In a few minutes we were in Peshawar and found that a direct train to Lahore was leaving in a hour. We saw nothing to keep us in Peshawar & the magnetism of India was getting stronger & stronger as we got nearer & nearer. We hassled around trying to decide how, what, & where to buy our tickets. This was a new experience — learning how to handle the Pakistani train system. A little bewildered & not sure what was our best move, we bought $3.50 ticket (1st class) for the 12 hour journey, wolfed down a quick 60¢ dinner & found a spot on the not-so-classy first class car.

Now we could really feel the magnetism of India. It was getting stronger and stronger as we got nearer and nearer. So we decided to skip Peshawar and try for a direct train to Lahore that was leaving in an hour. This was a whole new experience—learning how to handle the Pakistani train system. A little bewildered, we hustled around trying to decide how, what, and where to buy our tickets. We ended up buying first class tickets ($3.50, which promised padded seats), wolfed down a quick 60-cent dinner, and found a spot on the not-so-classy first-class car.

Our car was very crowded. I was happy to be near a window that blew in hot, muggy air. We pulled out almost on time, and I savored the breeze. The countryside was flat, lush, and interesting. I began reading Orwell's *Animal Farm*. It was good and the time passed nicely.

It didn't occur to me that we were riding a steam train until I found myself gazing at how beautiful the tiny flicks of black ash were as they landed on my glistening-with-sweat arm.

Then the sun set and the bugs came. The lights worked like on my old bike—the faster you go, the brighter they shine. This was not a very bright train. The bugs took an unfortunate liking to me and I made a bloody declaration: "Death by ruthless squashing to any bug that lands on me from now on." I decided that I would just mash them with my thumb or fingers and roll them through my arm and leg hairs until they disappeared—either rubbing into my skin or falling off. The ride dragged on and so did the bugs.

I finished *Animal Farm* and then began reading up on India. As we neared Lahore, the train got even more crowded, and Gene and I were lucky to have seats. This was our first taste of the kinds of beggars, cripples, religious singers, and crushing crowds that would be a routine part of train travel for the rest of the trip. But we got to our destination and that's what counts.

It was nearly midnight as we stepped into the muddy puddled streets of Lahore. The hotel situation looked bad, but luckily, I found a guy with a room for rent and a shower next door. (Gene didn't tell me about the lizards until later.) It was a hole, but it did serve its purpose. I took a cooling shower and found a comfortable spot among the bumps and curves of my cot. We turned the fan up to a gale and discussed what a wonderful saying "When the shit hits the fan" is. For some stupid reason, we were woken at 5:00 a.m. by the hotel guy because someone was complaining we were "roaming the hotel." Nonsense! And now we couldn't get any more good deep sleep.

Still, I was high-spirited. We'd arrived in Lahore, our last city in Pakistan, only minutes from the Indian border.

✻   ✻   ✻

Lahore was a tangle of people, horses, strange vehicles, and hot, muggy noise. We were lost without a map, so we caught a little funny three-wheeled motor rickshaw. The ride was crazy. We couldn't keep straight faces as we swerved in and out of traffic going both ways on all sides of the road. Rickshaw-ing through the chaos, we took it all in. Lahore is a ramshackle, "thrown-together," crazy city cluttered with insignificant vehicles, businesses, and fruit stands. There's rarely a dull moment for the wide-eyed visitor.

We stumbled off at the main street called "The Mall" and spent a few hours just wandering around, stopping for a bite to eat or sip a Coke—just experiencing this cultural center of Pakistan. Boy, is this place hot and muggy. Even a shower and the fan doesn't hide the humidity and stickiness. We checked out the Lahore Museum, really enjoying its statue of the "Fasting Buddha."

Now for Lahore's greatest sight. We were appropriately impressed by the huge structure that loomed before us—the Badshahi Mosque, one of the largest in the world.

At the entrance, we watched a changing of the guard that tried to be very impressive. Then I put on slippers and had a blanket wrapped around my indecent legs as we entered the vast courtyard of this Muslim holy spot. We climbed way up to the top of a minaret and got a spectacular view of low, flat, and sprawling Lahore. Then, careful not to trip over my modesty dress, I descended the tight spiral staircase and we crossed over to inspect the lackluster fort. I'm glad we stopped in Lahore, but we're getting antsy, because now we know we're going to India tomorrow.

In the park around the mosque, we got talking with a Pakistani about their relationship with India. Here's what I think I learned: When India won its independence from Britain it then had to deal with a divided society with a Hindu majority and a Muslim minority that didn't want to share a nation. After tragic fighting (as this guy told it), India's aggressive Hindus pushed most of India's Muslims into newly created Muslim countries carved out of India—East and West Pakistan. Gene and I both agreed that we would work very hard to understand this complicated culture, to give our visit a little more depth.

As we crazy-rickshawed back to our hotel, we had to work our way through a herd of water buffalo that easily could have pounded our rickety rickshaw into a puddle if they wanted to. But we made it, took another cold shower, and got ready for bed.

Most of our work was behind us and most of the adventure was ahead. We were at the doorstep of India.

We waited and waited for the bus. It was crucial for our spirits that we get into India today, and these borders are notorious for taking

*In Lahore, we hung out with
Pakistani med students in a
park and shared perspectives.*

a lot of time and simply closing down for the day. Ever since leaving Turkey, we've measured our Hippie Trail progress by how many borders were between us and India. Finally, this was the last border.

Fortunately, a nice old guy offered us a cheap taxi ride to the border and we jumped on it. After 30 minutes of weaving in and out of cattle and wild traffic, we reached the end of Pakistan. We stepped into the customs house, showed our passports, and were waved on. We walked a short way down a pleasant road without a soldier in sight. That's when it hit us: There was India.

India! Words can't explain my joy as I stepped across that happy tree-lined border. I dreamed so long to experience this enchanted sub-continent and now I was here. I know I could have just flown to India. But I'm glad I endured the overland road even though there were many moments, long moments, when I thought the whole idea was a stupid mistake and I dreamed of the good fun and food I could be enjoying in Greece or Italy. But now, as I walked among turbaned Sikhs, wallowing water buffalo, and lush green fields, I felt fantastic, beaming with a feeling of accomplishment, and my spirit soared.

I doubt if I'll ever do this trip this way again, but I experienced three rewarding and unforgettable weeks and learned so much about myself. Like finding a hidden door in a luxurious old library, I'd turned the key and the world opened up before me, rekindling my love of travel and showing me the rich rewards that were simply there for the taking.

Crossing the border into India,
I strangely felt like I was coming home.
Going from sparsely populated and
arid to densely populated and humid,
and from Islam to Hindustan, there
was a clear feeling that we were
crossing a big cultural divide.

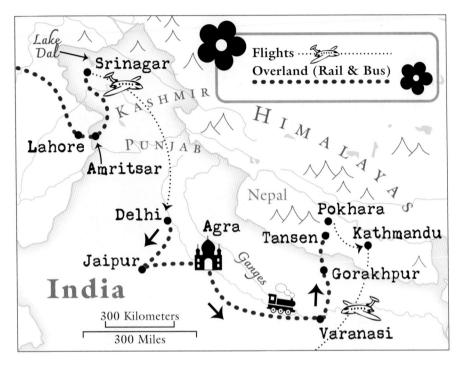

*Much of the Hippie Trail runs
through the great cities of India.*

We hopped into a minibus. Before long, it was filling up fast, and India was right in my face. The population density was inescapable: just when the bus seemed packed to the hilt, a man got on, picked up a stranger's child, and sat down with the child on his lap. So that's how they get along here.

Our first stop in India was Amritsar, the capital of the Punjab. The holy center of the Sikh religion, it is a jumbly city teeming with bicycle rickshaws and people.

We rickshawed over to the wondrous Golden Temple, the St. Peter's and Mecca of the Sikh religion. This was the most holy place for the Sikhs and, in keeping with their faith, they opened their doors with a heart-felt hospitality to anyone who visited. We had to wear a scarf over our heads and enter barefoot after washing our feet. Inside the massive square complex was a man-made lake and, in the middle, as if it was floating, was that golden island of Sikh holiness.

We wandered around soaking in all the exotic rituals and friendly people. Inside the island temple I saw a mysterious and very serious gathering of pilgrims and holy people. Music was played by a small orchestra, people were tossing coins, meditating, and taking a sort of communion. I was quite surprised that we were allowed to experience this room. I'll never forget that holy scene or that generous act of sharing it with two scruffy non-Sikh backpackers like us.

✻ ✻ ✻

Gene was still feeling lousy, so he sacked out while I went out to arrange for our ticket to Kashmir.

Gene needed a good night's sleep, so I grabbed the last berth on the first-class sleeper for him. There was one second-class reserved seat left, but the ticket booth was mobbed by Indians. What to do? I knew Western tourists often got preferred treatment, so I made friends with the assistant station master. After lots of running around, I had what I wanted. We would be leaving tonight.

I picked up Gene and we headed back to the station. All the way I was busy counseling our rickshaw boy—a curious and very eager-to-learn Sikh—on how to hustle American girls. By the time we got to the station, he learned to say, "How's it goin' baby?"

As we waited at the platform, I got my first sample of the famed Indian train-station food. I had a great meal of meat patties, fries, cooked vegetables, bread and butter, pudding, and a pot of tea filling me for well under a dollar. And that was the more expensive "Western" meal. You can live very cheap in India.

We located our reserved places. It was nice to see "Mr. Steves" written on the list outside the car. I said goodbye to Gene for the night as he settled into his first-class sleeper and I stepped into my second-class car.

In the process I bumped into Maria and Duncan and two other friends from the marathon Istanbul-Tehran bus ride. Asia is a huge continent but us hippie overlanders seem to stick together. It was great to see them. We shared our adventures since we parted in Tehran and chatted for a while. They were lucky to have sleeping berths.

I returned to my seat and readied my tailbone for a long over-night ride. I borrowed Maria's book on India and actually made several hours of the long ride interesting by diving into that book and getting a great background on India and Hinduism. With each stop of the train, I'd run out, soak my shirt, and have a quick Coke or tea. I kind of mentally turned the potential all-night-ordeal into an interesting personal challenge. And I carried out hundreds of death sentences on bugs that landed on me. Many will forever stain the pages of Maria's book. Finally, tired of sitting and ready to brave cockroaches and the unknown elements of the filthy floor, I stretched out on my poncho for a troubled hour or two of half-sleep and at 4:30 the train pulled to a stop.

It was still dark as we groggily stepped off the train and followed the crowd to await our connecting bus to Kashmir. I stretched out on the cement, covered every inch of my body with spare clothes to escape the bugs, and slept for an hour until the 7 a.m. all aboard.

Soon we were sitting in the bouncy back seat of our rickety "A class" bus where we would spend 12 hours winding through treacherous mountain roads to the hidden land of Kashmir.

The bus made good time considering its age and the condition of the terrain we had to cross. It was 200 miles of almost continuously winding switchback narrow roads spiced with dreadful cliffs, huge falling boulders, local natives, lots of trucks and military vehicles, and constant signs reminding drivers with tacky little rhymes and slogans like "Drive carefully—your family needs you" or "Better late than dead."

Ooo! I was excited. Not even feeling my lack of sleep, I enjoyed the ride. Everyone seemed to be headed north to escape the mucky heat of India and find happiness in the blissful valley of Kashmir. The scenery was dramatic and I soaked up the fun conversation my British friends, Maria and Duncan, had to offer. I really enjoy something about Maria, but I guess that's just too bad.

The countryside was lush and green—almost tropical. I knew right away that this was my kind of place. By mid-afternoon we went through a very long one-lane tunnel and when we popped out, we were greeted by a majestic view of the huge valley that substantiated the claims about paradise. Kashmir was dreamy. The landscape was mystically beautiful like the seductive landscape behind Mona Lisa that I've long wanted to explore.

The wild and windy road became a drive through a garden that had me thinking maybe Dubrovnik was being replaced by Kashmir as my ideal place for a romantic honeymoon. After a couple more hours, we pulled into Srinagar, the Venice of India. A cheery sign greeted us as we arrived: "Welcome to Kashmir—you are now in Paradise."

"Welcome to Kashmir - You're now in Paridise".
Then we were struck by a view of the huge
valley that substantiated the claim about paradise.
This place was dreamy. The landscape was
mystically beautiful like the fantastic fuzzy
landscapes that typically make the background
of paintings of the Madonna like the Mona Lisa.
This valley - so far away from everything was
worthy of any praise anybody ever gave it.
   The wild & windy road became a drive
through a garden and I thought maybe
Dubrovnik was being replaced by Kashmir as the
ideal place for a romantic honeymoon.
   After a couple more hours we pulled into Srinagar,
the Venice of North India and just like the guides'
warned, we were surprised by very desperate houseboat

give us & we pretended to be impressed - not
really caring too much about the price as much as
about the quality. We read the rave reviews
some of his previous American guests gave him
& agreed to the healthy price of 80 rupees for
the double with dinner, breakfast, tea & a family of
literal servants. I knew we were giving him a
very good price but I also knew that when you
pay well for something like this you reap the
benefits of a true first class product.
  Sitting topside on the _____ Gene & I sipped
tea with cracke_____ _____ darkened out
boats of all kinds glided quietly by below us.
  This was what _____ dreamed of & what I had
been waiting for. 25 days ago I left rainy Savonlinna
in the middle of Finland and I knew I had a
long road to _____ Even then, my sights were
set _____ _____ rthwest corner of India.
_____ _____ tea & I

Kashmir

August 7
August 13

*Kashmir, where India meets
Tibet, is a wondrous place.*

It was like Paradise Found. Sitting topside on the sundeck of our houseboat, Gene and I sipped tea with crackers as the red sky darkened and boats of all kinds glided quietly by below us. This was what I had dreamed of and what I had been waiting for.

Twenty-five days ago, I left rainy Scandinavia and I knew I had a long road to travel. Even then, my dreams were set on Srinagar in the mountainous northwest corner of India. Finally, I'm sitting on my houseboat, sipping my tea, and I will be very busy from now on, just relaxing and enjoying myself. Never have I worked so hard or traveled so long for a single moment. And this perch in enchanting Kashmir was well worth it.

But pristine paradise still needs to be earned.

No sooner had we had pulled into Srinagar, just like the guidebooks warned, we were swamped by desperate houseboat owners eager to rent their cheap places to stay. Fighting our way through, determined to just get some info first, we were claimed by one "boat lord" and whisked away in a three-wheeled scooter to the dock and onto a luxurious, long water taxi, kind of like a Venetian gondola with a canopy bed. This guy offered us the world, including a free first night, but we didn't like the pressure job he put on us. So, I hailed another boat and with some difficulty, we excused ourselves to get a more thorough review of the Srinagar scene.

Several boats down the way, we stopped at a cute looking houseboat with a vacancy sign out. The neighboring boats had very, very comfortable laid-back and relaxed-looking tourists just lazing around and savoring the leisurely life that abounds here. The owner came running over and we were quite impressed by his boat and his style. He gave us the old line about the secret price he would give us and we pretended to be impressed—not really caring too much about the price as much as about the quality. We read the rave reviews some of his previous American guests gave him and agreed to the healthy price of 80 rupees ($5) for the double with dinner, breakfast, tea, and a family of literal servants. We could have chiseled on the price but how could we complain? I knew that when you pay well for something like this, you reap the benefits of a truly first-class product and can command a good return. I like to ask for plenty of tea, get my filthy clothes washed, be able to borrow the houseboat's *shikara* (little Kashmiri gondola) when I want it, and still feel like I'm making a family's day financially.

We closed the deal, and soon we were checked in and lounging on the sundeck.

Then the houseboy stopped by to tell us that the hot water was prepared and we could shower before our duck dinner was ready. After our showers, we were presented with roast duck, cooked potatoes, carrots, rice, sweet and cooked apples in syrup, a wonderful Persian tea, and water that the man said he boiled and was safe to drink. We feasted while the man stood next to the table beaming with pride for the meal and making sure that our every need was attended to. That made me a bit uncomfortable, but India is a culture of hard class divisions and staying here, you've got servants whether you want them or not. This was a family show and I guess this one family had run this houseboat for generations—probably serving rich British bureaucrats who ruled India back in the 1800s.

Our houseboat has a little veranda overlooking the canal, a richly furnished living room with a small dining table, two double

Muzaffar's, our floating—and
luxurious for us—home in Kashmir

On the streets of Srinagar

bedrooms, and two bathrooms, and on top is a pleasant sun deck where we can watch the Kashmiri world float by.

As boats paddled by, crickets chirped, and Kashmiris argued noisily across the canal, I sat in the living room sipping sweet Persian tea and collecting my thoughts in this journal. I'm looking forward to becoming at-home in Kashmir.

❊   ❊   ❊

I slept exactly eight good hours. After a lavish breakfast of hot cereal with oat milk, toast, egg, and tea, we caught a *shikara* to the "Mainland." I had the *shikara* boy take the long way, paddling us through the many canals lined with houseboats of all classes—from half-sunk, rotten rafts to virtual floating palaces.

We headed out to Ali Kadal—the old part of Srinagar.

Srinagar was exciting, colorful, a weave of both busy and lazy people, and a trip just to walk through. We ambled aimlessly, capturing memories like butterflies. This is where old men sat cross-legged in doorways that look like windowsills, engulfed in their big Korans (Kashmir is mostly Muslim), boys climbed like monkeys around streetlamps and roof tops, cows munched newspapers in the streets, and onion-sellers handled mobs of hungry customers.

The buildings were ornately carved wood, aged and darkened after countless hot summers and violent winters. Mosques rose above the tangled skyline and trembling bridges crossed Jhelum River. (I have a hunch that describing these awesome sights adequately after I get home, even with the help of photographs, will be frustrating.)

We wandered into a neighborhood of ramshackle houses, torn-apart streets, dusty horses, and what looked to me like ruins left by a war. Not wanting to linger there, we walked to the edge of town where we were met by a long-bearded, dignified old gentleman who spoke very good English. He introduced himself, saying he wasn't a businessman, he worked for the hospital. Then he showed us a photograph of him from the 1940s in the hospital. After walking with us for a while, he gave us the pitch we should have known was coming, and I signed his book donating 2 rupees to the hospital.

Srinagar was a fun place—lots of Indians there on vacation wearing outfits as varied as their vast and diverse country. (I like to think of India as diverse culturally and linguistically as Europe.) There were inviting parks, chaotic intersections, plenty of street sellers, and more than enough craft shops. At a bookstore, I picked up a *"lern-to-spell"* book that looked like it *mite* work. We ran into our old Hippie Trail friends, Maria and Duncan, at a classic old Indian coffeehouse. Having coffee sparked my coffee tasters and I realized how long it had been since I had a good cup of "joe."

Then we dealt with some important business. We went to the Air India office to book our plane tickets for our next destination, Delhi. The office was noisy and crowded, but I made my way to the desk and got two youth tickets (25% discount) for $30 each, which was great.

Then we made our way to the Government Central Market. I planned to get all my shopping out of the way. Shopping on the road is a waste of a good sightseeing day, but it's kind of a necessary evil.

The Central Market was 60 or 80 shops in a large square all with fixed and government-regulated prices. I didn't have the energy today to do a lot of bargaining, so this was my safest bet. I got three hand-woven pillow covers with happy patterns (I'm thinking a little bit domestically for post-college life), some papier mâché hand-painted boxes, and another little fox fur "purselette" that, when draped around my chin, makes a crazy full beard that matches my hair.

We headed home, ferried by my favorite crazy singing and jabbering *shikara* boy. He told me all about his lucky raffle tickets while I did most of the paddling. The other guests on our houseboat had checked out, so now we had the boat to ourselves and we moved into the best room with that all-important sit-down toilet.

Gene and I went up on the roof, and under the sun we had

Our fruits and vegetables came to us.

The neighborhood was filled with
floating guesthouses for rent.

a snack: some delicate Persian tea with Kashmiri bread. Surveying boats, long and narrow, laden with anything you could want, float by servicing anyone who wants service, we thought you could spend weeks here and never leave the boat. Across the canal is a small jungle inhabited by a large local family letting us observe life going on the way it has for centuries. Birds and bats fly by, dark tanned and naked children paddle happily through the lily pads. And out back the owner and his family live in a modest little boat quite apart from our touristy world, but ready to do whatever we ask.

I hope this lifestyle doesn't permanently corrupt me. It's worth the risk.

⁂ ⁂ ⁂

Gene and I borrowed our boat's ancient *shikara,* got a second paddle, and set out to explore Lake Dal. At first, the going was hard and slow. We were fighting a bit of a wind and neither of us were very good with this sleek but difficult old boat. Little boys floated by solo, paddling faster than the both of us, but this was fun…humbling but fun. We were on our own, free to mosey in and out of lagoons lined with traditional boat families doing their fascinating thing. The nicest thing about it was no one could try to help us or sell us things—we were un-pestered…and free to explore.

Working hard, we made our way through the houseboat neighborhoods and out into the wide open of Lake Dal. We docked on a "swimming boat." A guy "parked" our boat for us and we stripped down to our underwear and enjoyed a fun, if not refreshing, swim. The water was so warm—I was actually cooler in the shade.

I went for a fantastic round of water skiing. What a thrill, waterskiing under the lush Himalayas and the Kashmir blue skies. I skied with abandon and had a blast whipping along to the side of the speed boat, jumping the wake, and going around and around. Later I tried and failed to get up on one ski. I tried getting up on two and kicking one off but failed miserably. I could feel the altitude here—I was exhausted.

After lounging around and splitting an apple juice, our boat was fetched, and off we rowed. Our *shikara* drew only a few inches and had no keel so we had a hard time steering a straight course. Every few minutes we'd clumsily do a 360-degree circle, probably much to the entertainment of the local boaters nearby.

We checked out a garden isle, bought an apple from a floating general store—more for the memory than the apple. We enjoyed the novel experience of having a nude and beautiful girl frolicking around our stern. And then as the sun set, we returned home, tired, a bit sunburned and ready for lunch.

Reaching our once-friendly houseboat, we noticed the mood had changed. We'd mentioned to the owner that we'd be checking out soon. Now that we were leaving, our boat man was cutting back on the service. In fact, the servants were almost mutinous. We asked him to send a *shikara* to pick up our friends and he refused! Our lunch was a rather meager stew with old bread. I thought he had class, but he was getting on me.

In fact, all along this Hippie Trail, there was a standard of gouging Westerners whenever possible. While it got tiresome, it did get me thinking about the gap between the First World and the Third World. Even scruffy backpackers like us had more money than most locals. So, I guess this playful battle between us was just part of life on the road. We assumed their anger was part of the show and we did our best to stay good natured about it all. The main thing for us, though: we needed to be sure our money would last as long as our trip. Money was like gas in our tank. And if we ran out, we couldn't get home.

It's funny, when you're treated like a king you begin to expect it and when the "servants" let you down, it takes a little bit of adjusting.

After a pot of tea, we took off to enjoy the famous gardens that visitors to Kashmir have been enjoying for centuries.

From our houseboat in Srinagar,
Kashmir, we can observe life going
on the way it has for centuries.

Shikara on Nagin Lake

Working our way around Lake Dal, our first stop was the lavish Oberoi Palace Hotel. Many hotels put the word "palace" in their name, but only a few deserve it, and the Oberoi is one. We marched in like we belonged and snooped around. The only thing we could afford was the wonderful bathrooms. I swiped a roll of quality toilet paper for the good of our world and we said goodbye.

Next, we were at Gardens. Built by and fit for a king, I can imagine all the romantic hanky-panky that must have rustled these graceful branches. We took a snooze but soon the ants were playing Gulliver with me. After a nice cake and tea, I got a diarrhea attack and, in frantic silence, I found a hidden corner of the garden and fertilized.

Our final stop was the famous Shalimar Gardens. In this lush valley, this colorful park of gardens, flowers, and tumbling water stood out. Seeing all the Indians—both local and tourists from the south—coming here to relax and picnic was part of the Shalimar experience.

As the sun set, we stayed for the romantic Shalimar Gardens sound-and-light show. We foolishly bought first-class tickets (it didn't make any difference—just cost double), and quickly sank back into the Mughal Empire (1600s) as lights and sound brought the sexy garden dreamily alive. The moon shone, the trees were silhouetted, and colorful lights and historic stories helped me imagine what these gardens might have been like before the arrival of Europeans. I enjoyed the lighting, fountains, and Indian music.

Happy but exhausted, we realized we were miles from home. It was hard to get a taxi for a reasonable price. We snagged a three-wheel rickshaw and, with no time to bicker, we got in and jumbled along Lake Dal toward home. Halfway there, I had our driver stop, shut off the motor, and we sat for a moment in lovely silence on the moonlit bank of Lake Dal. This is a very special valley and I will return.

Pony ride in the Himalayas? Let's! We caught an early bus to Gulmarg, one of India's high mountain resorts. Our plan was to hire horses and ride up from remote Gulmarg to even more remote Khilanmarg, at 9,000 feet.

This was a "tourist" bus, but at least it was filled mostly with Indian tourists, very few were European. We climbed into a lush forest crawling with monkeys. Monkeys wild in the forest! They ogle the bus and then scamper away—often with a baby clinging to their back.

The moment we arrived in Gulmarg all the pony men gathered noisily around our bus, showing cards and credentials as we stepped off. We chose an old man assisted by a young man and had to accept their 20-rs-per-pony price to go up to Khilanmarg and back. We wanted to ride alone, but Gene got a more difficult horse and the old man followed us, which turned out to be nice because the trail was hard to follow in places and the old man was a little security for us.

I was a bit cautious on my horse, Ginger. I broke my arm once falling off a pony and I was carrying my camera and zoom lens which would never survive a fall. There was no horn on Ginger's saddle but it offered a little leather flap to hang on to instead. We began to climb and the trail got muddy and rocky. The going was slow and difficult, and I had this terrible image of Ginger slipping, falling, and crushing my leg beyond recognition. We made our way up the lousy trail through dramatic scenery and after four kilometers, we reached

Heading to Khilanmarg, Gene
got a more difficult horse.

I've never met a family so disconnected from the rest of the world...or so warm and welcoming.

Khilanmarg. The old man got a tow most of the way up hanging onto Gene's pony's tail.

Khilanmarg was rugged, thin-air beauty—an open meadow high above the placid valley of Kashmir and bordered by towering mountains. Cows grazed among the rocks and a few trees and rustic shacks, and there were three or four tents set up to serve the handful of tourists—all Indian—tea and coffee. We sat under the tent through a short rainstorm. The clouds kept us from viewing the Himalayas and Nanga Parbat, the world's ninth-highest mountain. Gene had Nescafé and I ate some peanuts we've been carrying since Iran.

Then, unencumbered by camera equipment or lousy trails, Ginger and I went galloping happily across the meadows—unforgettable. While Ginger at a gallop was majestic, Ginger in a canter was more of a comedy. I was popping up and down like a cross between a pogo stick and a jackhammer. What fun! If I only had a little more confidence in the saddle, it would have been even better.

On the far side of the meadow, I came to a cozy-looking dwelling made of stacked stones. Animal pelts hung on a tree outside, sleds leaned on the wall, quietly awaiting the first winter snowfall. I couldn't pass it up. I rode up, hitched Ginger to a post, and introduced myself to some children who invited me inside.

It was like entering a time-passed world. Not a trace of the 20th century could be found, nor the 19th or 18th. Really! This was a pure look at life in the wilds. The father was sleeping on leaves but woke up with a gleam in his eyes and a warm handshake. The mother was kneading bread next to an earthen fire that filled the hut with a warm, smokey feeling and a good smell. Rays of light shone through cracks in the rocks landing on the happy faces of the long-haired and freckled children. Their clothes were dirty and their hair was unwashed, but nothing struck me as unclean. They were totally detached from any outside influence, yet it seemed like a comfortable existence. I'll never forget sitting on the rustic bench under the thatched roof next to the beautiful teenage girls and in front of the simple fireplace-stove. Without a hint of begging, they seemed noble, at peace, and simply happy to meet us.

I imagine they would remember my visit as long as I would.

* * *

Back down in Srinagar, it was hot, and we decided that rather than stay in town we would try and find another houseboat on nearby Nagin Lake.

After several "Sorry, we're full"s and getting a feeling like this lake was for diplomats, rich Germans, and honeymooners only, we found "The Ritz." On the outside it was nothing special, lacking the highly varnished, ornately carved exterior of other boats, but inside it was lavish and spacious—really the Ritz. We had a spacious double bedroom with soft beds, western toilet, fancy carved wood paneling, Persian carpet, ornately-framed mirrors, and, of course, a view. The dining room had high royal-type chairs, old English dinnerware, and plenty of boiled drinking water. The living room was just as good with comfortable chairs and a sofa, lots of books and magazines, and a sunny back patio. I love paging through old guest books—and this family's told their boat's story going back to the 1920s.

We sipped tea up on the sun deck. We were impressed with the peaceful location in the marshy shore of Nagin Lake among high reeds and lots of birds, with a gorgeous view of the fort and the mountains. I made a study of the ever-changing Kashmiri world around us. All kinds of boats glided by. I got a local newspaper from one merchant—thankful that English is the language of commerce and tourism throughout India. We watched ducks paddle by and birds dive-bomb for fish. *Shikaras* and boats of all kinds ornamented the lake and, as the sun set, they became romantic silhouettes under a streaky pink-orange sky. We enjoyed the view until the moon shone brightly.

The "Pony Men" of Gulmarg

Relaxing at "The Ritz"
on Nagin Lake

I'm determined to relax and restore my energy to 110%, because from the minute we leave here, we'll be going full-bore and taking in as much as we possibly can. But for now, on our last day in Kashmir, we stuck to the plan: we did nothing. Today is the nothing day. Intensive nothing and relaxation. I laid up on the sun deck, cooled off under the shower, laid in bed to dry, wrote a postcard or two, flipped through some old *Newsweeks* in the living room, and sat on the steps heading down to the water from the back deck looking at little fish and watching ducks gobble them up.

Lunch was the best meal so far, with tender goat meat and cooked vegetables. I sighed afterward and laid down for a short rest. I opened my window and, motionless, let the sun warm my bed.

We spent the remainder of the afternoon reading, writing, sunbathing, and just enjoying the fantastic setting we found ourselves in. Up on the sundeck, I enjoyed watching the lake life go by: the French couple next to us rolling suspicious-looking cigarettes and feeding breadcrumbs to hungry ducks, two men pulling a clumsy houseboat down the canal, the local family across the way carrying on like there were no tourists and this wasn't the 20th century, and big carnivorous birds—silhouetted by the setting sun—making the wispy trees sway. Nibbling on our roast duck dinner, I thought you could never leave this perch and write poems all day long.

But tonight's our last night here in Kashmir and we're both ready to get on with our trip. For the rest of our trip, it will be go, go, go. Tomorrow, we kick off the next major phase of this adventure, plunging deep into the heart of India.

August 14th, Monday   Srinagar — Delhi

We woke up for the last time in Kashmir happy to be
flying out. After a disappointing breakfast the servant asked
me, "Food is good?" For once I was frank & said, "Not really."
   We packed said goodbye & caught a boat ashore. I
wanted to do a little shopping but the Gov't Emporium did'
open until 10:00 so Gene & I sat around writing post c
& wishing we had taken the early morning flight.
   At 11:00 our bus rolled out, packed with people re
fly to Delhi. The airport was deffinately" small- to
we were tick   to be flying to Delhi and avoid
long overland   ney.
   As I we   ough the security check they ask
I had a knif   I did & I had to check it
was funny to   that ju   like another pre
as say goodby   it hop   I would see
Army knife   in   It jo   the
of Samurai   toy   tols & s
potential h   king te
   Our Boein   7 was   ite full
in row 17   behind   wing.
they meant   snacks   will be
flight. I c   use   big's
up & by a   1:00 w   ere air
the puffy   above
valley. It s
     re

India

August 14

August 28

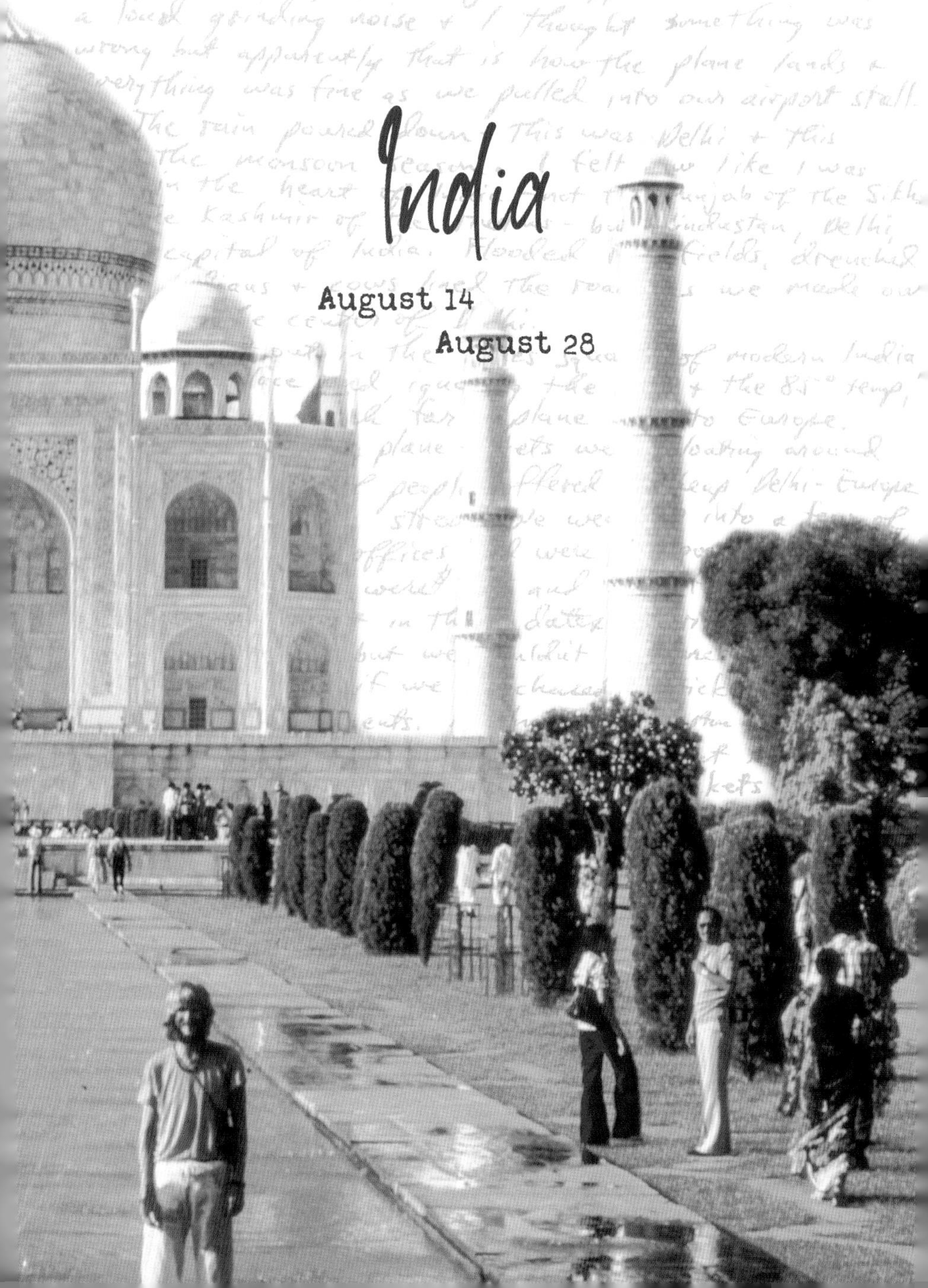

*At Lakshmi Narayan Temple
in Delhi, India*

Contrast swizzles a travel experience...it brings out the flavor. At least that's what I tried to convince myself as we caught a plane to trade our mountain paradise for urban Indian intensity. The propellers of our Dutch-made Fokker turned over like they have for decades and soon we were airborne, climbing through the puffy broken clouds and above our restful Kashmir Valley.

As the mountains gave way to a vast and fertile plain, we flew over a flooded India. The countryside was lush, green, and thriving in the life-giving waters of the rainy season. They've been having the wettest monsoon in 70 years, and it was evident. I've looked at a map before and wondered why India has no lakes, but now I see that during the monsoon season, half of India *is* a lake.

The wording on the sign on the seatback, "Life vest your underseat," failed to make me feel safe. I ventured back to the plane's toilet. Going down the aisle was like walking on a trampoline and using it was like sitting in an airborne outhouse. An old decal showed a stick figure demonstrating how, to use this toilet, you don't stand on the rim and squat over it. You actually sit *on* the rim. I enjoyed a view of the rain-soaked Indian countryside below through the hole (another first for me). Bombs away! I hope I don't get lockjaw from the rusty lid.

Back in my seat, the stewardess with a red-dotted forehead and a powerful smile sari-d down the aisle handing out sweets and "freshies." What a lovely alternative to surface travel! And cheap! This is a new experience for me—enjoying air travel for what you'd expect to pay for a bus ride. But remember: "Life vest your underseat."

It was monsoon season in Delhi and the rain poured down. Drenched dark Indians (it seems the lower, poorer castes have darker skin—and they're the ones stuck out in the downpour) and pampered cows lined the flooded roads as we made our way to the center of Delhi. Ignoring the rain and the 85-degree temperature, we got to the "Times Square" of modern India, Connaught Place, and checked into our room at the YMCA.

I felt now like I was really in the heart of India—not the Punjab of the Sikhs or the disputed Kashmir of the Muslims—but Hindustan, Delhi, the capital of India.

Curious to explore Delhi, we spent a few hours walking around this city of four million. First, we plunged into Old Delhi, which was really refreshing. We wide-eyed our way through crowded streets, working our way deep into the dark and fragrant innards of the bazaar. We watched cigarettes being rolled by hand—tobacco wrapped in a leaf that sold for 3 cents a pack, sat in to observe some fancy embroidery work, ducked through jungles of silk saris and glittering sashes, dodged hurried bicycle rickshaws, peered down dark alleys, and had some fun with a photogenic sign that read simply, "Sex Disorders."

Today is India's Independence Day. Thirty-one years ago, they broke away from England. We were hoping for an exciting day full of "Fourth of July"-type activities, but there was nothing much going on. Most attractions were just closed. So, we designed the rest of our day to see parks, monuments, and things that were open all the time.

Starting down Parliament Road, we passed through the communications nerve center for India to the Parliament building and an impressive, expansive area of parks and royal-type buildings. A long avenue, Rajpath, led to the famous India Gate with the eternal flame for WWI victims. We took a three-wheeled rickshaw to India Gate and were greeted by flexing cobras and dancing bears.

Photogenic sign in Old Delhi

*With poverty woven into everyday
life, this trip gave me a new kind
of souvenir: indelible images and
important questions to struggle with.*

Not really in the mood for dancing bears, we caught a rickshaw to the Lodi Tombs Park—a lovely, very green park dotted with old, ruined tombs. Sitting on a log, we were entertained by a family of cute little dressed-up and trained monkeys.

We then wandered into a large group of Sikhs all dressed up at a religious picnic. We enjoyed their choral group with the same wind-powered keyboard instrument and drums that we heard in the Amritsar temple. Sikhs are amazing people—productive, hardworking, prosperous, clean, proud, and devoted. They never cut their hair or beard but are sure to wash it every day. They wear proud turbans, and feel they have a strong bond wherever they are scattered. They are also quite evangelical and made sure we got all the info we needed. (Tonight for bedtime reading we will find out why we should become Sikhs.)

Then we caught a scooter to the zoo, which was packed and festive. The monsoon clouds were gathering so everyone was busy enjoying the disappearing sun while they could. There were lots of exotic animals and even some ducks that came all the way from America! It was a vast yet sparsely populated zoo with sleepy hot animals scattered thinly around. I saw a lethargic tiger, peered right down a gross hippo's mouth—cavernous as a giant garbage can—and saw kangaroos hop just like in cartoons. Then the monsoon hit and everyone—both animals and people—took refuge under the nearest tree. Standing under a friendly notice "Passing of urine not allowed," we calmly waited for the rain to stop.

After it did, we stopped by the Free Church of Delhi. I hadn't been to a Christian service all summer. We walked in during a hymn and found a small, mostly Indian, congregation singing while the organist fumbled along under a whirling fan. Then the woman pastor in a snow-white veiled outfit read the lessons with a strict Puritan manner and a terse English accent. Her strength and dedication were impressive. It must be hard to run a Christian church in a land so

We woke up for the last time in Kashmir happy to be flying out. After a disappointing breakfast the servant asked me, "Food is good?" For once I was frank & said, "Not really".

We packed, said goodbye & caught a boat ashore. I wanted to do a little shopping but the Gov't Emporium didn't open until 10:00 so Gene & I sat around writing post cards & wishing we had taken the early morning flight.

At 11:00 our bus rolled out, packed with people ready to fly to Delhi. The airport was "deffinately" "small-town" but we were tickled to be flying to Delhi and avoid the long long overland journey.

As I went through the security check they asked me if I had a knife. I did & I had to check it separately. It was funny to try that just like another piece of baggage as say goodby to it hoping I would see my dear Swiss Army knife again in Delhi. It joined the small pile of samurai swords, toy pistols & small knives - all potential hi-jacking tools.

Our Boeing 737 was quite full as we took our seats in row 17 just behind the wing. I wondered just what they meant by "snacks" will be served during the flight. I could use some big "snacks". We buckled up & by about 1:00 we were air-borne climing through the puffy broken clouds & above our restfull Kashmir valley. It served it's purpose. We had a great week & now, rested we are ready to finish the trip.

I was disappointed, not seeing a single Himalayain mountain but I felt very good watching the mountains below us flit easily by & I thought how nice it is not to be on a rickity old bus down there.

Snacks came - sandwich, cake, & fresh apple juice and I could have eaten more but one hour after we left we were descending into the capital of India - Delhi

They have been having the worst monsoon in 70 years and it was evident by the flooding we saw as we neared the ground. Then we vanished into a white cloud. I could see nothing but the wing out

the window. It was scary to thing we were going
400 or 500 blind miles per hour. Then we dropped
below the clouds + landed with a loud rumble. A
rear part of one of the jets flipped over making
a loud grinding noise + I thought something was
wrong but apparently that is how the plane lands +
everything was fine as we pulled into our airport stall.

The rain poured down - This was Delhi + this
was the monsoon season. I felt now like I was
really in the heart of India - not the Punjab of the Sikhs
or the Kashmir of the Muslims - but Hindustan, Delhi,
the capital of India. Flooded rice fields, drenched
dark Indians + cows lined the roads as we made our
way to the center of Delhi.

We got out in the "Times Square" of modern India,
Connaught Place and, ignoring the rain + the 85° temp,
we began our search for a plane ride to Europe.
Like people told us, plane tickets were floating around
everywhere. Lots of people offered us cheap Delhi-Europe
flights right on the street. We went up into a few of
the sleazy travel offices and were told good news - flights
to London or Paris were $335 and Frankfurt for $380-400.
They were consistent in their dates + prices so they
sounded reliable but we couldn't be sure + we would
be a bit uneasy if we purchased a ticket from one
of these shady agents. Air India or Pan Am were no
help to us but we did find the Student Travel
Bureau + they could sell us reliable tickets at the
same price. Now we had to decide which was better -
flying to London on the 5th of Sept for $332 or to
Frankfurt on the 6th of $400. Plan one would give us
2 days in London but we'd still have to buy the ticket
to Frankfurt + we didn't know what that would
cost. Plan 2 would be simpler, we'd have an extra
day in India but we'd have a dull day and a half to blow
in Frankfurt. We will chew this over + probably
decide on London by Wednesday.

With that completed we worked on a hotel. Delhi
wasn't a hick country town + a decent place would
cost us. We checked out several before we checked
into the YMCA. A spartan double room, good bathrooms
+ breakfast cost 43 R each. ($5.40)

permeated by Hindu and Buddhist traditions. I met some very nice people and, as a bonus, afterward I got a lecture from an herbal doctor evangelical about the seriousness of venereal disease. VD is the last of my worries here, unless you can pick it up from the rickshaw seats.

Back at our YMCA hotel, we have a feud building between us and the waiters and it gets worse with each meal. The root of the problem is probably our strange dining habits. We need our coffee or tea with, not after, the meal. We need water, preferably in a pitcher, so we can put our iodine in it. I eat my rice out of their serving bowl with milk and sugar. If we get up to get the water jug ourselves or find some sugar, they really get shook up. We keep demanding service, and they keep trying not to give it. I think there's a certain element of pride and stubbornness involved. But the food is clean, cheap, and edible, so we continue to eat and feud with our waiters at the Delhi YMCA.

I had a good, long shower and then—as if to get a little dose of home early—Gene and I invented a baseball game where we crumpled up pieces of paper and lobbed them into the swinging blades of the ceiling fan. If it fell through cleanly, it was a strike, if it got whacked it was a hit. Depending on which wall was hit, it could be a single, double, or triple. After three innings, Tissue led the Wrinkles, 3 to 2. We didn't make it to the 7th inning stretch. With the fan blowing hot and muggy air on me, I fell asleep.

※　※　※

Yesterday was the wettest day of India's year and today was only a little better.

We caught a bus tour of the main sights—thankful that India's common language for tourism is English. First, the Qutub Minar. With a tall, impressive tower and the first mosque in India, it was built around a mysterious iron pillar. Just then, the monsoon ripped loose, and we had no choice but to get drenched. It's so hot and sweaty, it's like stepping out of a shower with my clothes on.

My first real major Hindu temple,
Lakshmi Narayan Temple

सच पर विश्वास रखो
सच ही सोचो सच ही करो
BELIEVE IN TRUTH
THINK TRUTH &
LIVE TRUTH

The inspirational Mahatma Gandhi was just one of many threads woven into the fabric of Indian society.

We drove on to Humayun's Tomb, which predated Shah Jahan's Taj Mahal and kind of inspired it. We saw the Gandhi Museum. The Red Fort, built by the Mughal rulers, descendants of Genghis Khan, was huge, strong, and of course, red.

The highlight was Delhi's Lakshmi Narayan Temple. This was my first real major Hindu temple, and I really was fascinated by it. At the entrance, accompanied by a rag-tag band of temple musicians, several people gathered to pray. The architecture was unique, like nothing I'd ever seen before, and the gods and goddesses were eerily captivating. Respectfully barefoot, through the puddles I wandered, swept away by uncountable statuettes, paintings, mini shrines, devout pilgrims, and hypnotic music.

Later, with the rain persisting, we took in the National Museum. This big place was quite dull and, with signs like "Avoid touching. Keep yourself away," just not very inviting. We skipped the free 2:30 p.m. film, which would probably just be the museum again but on the screen—even duller! The sculptures seemed so crude next to Classical Greek or Roman works from the same centuries. I hope I'm not guilty of ethnocentrism.

Outside we had an impossible time, for some reason, securing an available rickshaw. Finally, we gave up and walked to a bus stop and hopped on, not knowing where it was going but at least it was going somewhere. As I suspected, it went to the hub, Connaught Place, where we went to the Kwality Restaurant expecting a kwality lunch. But no.

I've been so lucky for so long health-wise. Now suddenly, I felt worse than I had at any time yet on this trip. I figured now it was my turn. With a miserable stomach, kind of constipated, and even with a fever, all I wanted to do was lie under the fan.

Lying there, I admitted to myself that, someday, I would like to be able to travel in first-class style: taxis instead of scooters, screwdrivers instead of "Limca" (the local 7-Up), air-conditioning instead of fans, and Intercontinentals instead of YMCAs. But, as that dream requires dollars instead of cents, and a successful businessman instead of the income of a piano teacher, I steered myself away from those fantasies and back into my humble 23-year-old economic reality.

We passed the time with a strange and funny English-language Delhi newspaper, laughing at the esoteric crossword puzzle clues (e.g., "Direction for a parachutist with a dicky heart, about to play a snooker shot") and the matrimony section of the classifieds ("Homely daughter of millionaire, 165 cm, caste no bar") and minor headlines ("Tribesmen flog a vehicle, we hear").

After dinner, we caught a scooter and in 10 minutes we were inside the cool, modern, rich Oberoi Intercontinental Hotel for some Indian folk music and dance. Just then there was a power outage and they had to light up the little emergency candles—stubby from past outages. We occupied ourselves with a study of the Indian high society class. Beautiful girls, wealthy men, and proud Sikhs—with their turbans and chin-strap beards—filled the hall. Then, after a great rooftop view of Delhi spreading under the hazy setting sun, we sat down in the front row, psyched.

The tabla, harmonium, flute, and sitar started happily in. Each player was very aware of the others and subtlety was the key. Then we were treated to six or eight lovely Indian folk dances from all different regions of India. I always thought Indian dance was somber and serious, but these were gay, goofy, and spirited, kind of like American folk dances. The dancers and musicians were having a good time, getting into it, and I think having a few private jokes on the very touristy audience. I really enjoyed it. And Gene and I suddenly found ourselves fantasizing about buying a sitar.

On the rickshaw home, we talked about the concert and got into a pretty heavy discussion about cultural virtues and what is "cultured." We tried comparing the mountain shepherds we visited back in Kashmir to high society locals we sat with in the concert and with noted American poets and intellectuals back home. We both agreed that our eyes have definitely been opened by the complexity of our world on this trip-of-a-lifetime that we were sharing.

Now, after such a long day, all we wanted to do was go upstairs, lie down in our quiet room, and stare at the hypnotic ceiling fan. We did. Zzzzzz.

We both needed a good dose of village India. Rather than another day of the relatively big-city-modernness of Delhi, we wanted a more rural experience…an extra blast of the kind of raw Hippie Trail adventure we've experienced so many times in the last month.

Our goal: to check out an Indian village…a village that had never seen a Westerner in person…a place unmentioned in any travelers' guidebook. At the University of Washington, I was allowed to design my own class which I called "Village India." Today, I wanted to actually see things I had studied.

Unlike my UW professor, everyone in Delhi tried to talk us out of visiting a village. They said it was bad during the monsoon and not very interesting. Their pleas were actually counter-productive. We both really wanted a close look at a typical village.

We could have gone to a central terminal and caught a direct bus, but we wanted a village too small to be a stop on a main bus line. Instead, we rickshawed to the Delhi-Agra highway and hitched and bused along the road. I relish the challenge of getting somewhere the hard way—just taking anything rolling in the general direction and working my way confidently along the road until I reach my destination. Gene warily cautions me, "I don't know if anything will stop." But one man did, and after a pleasant and airy ride in the back of his truck, we said goodbye at the cut-off.

We headed down the dusty road, looking for a charming little hamlet called Molarband. India is basically a village society, with only about 15% of its massive population residing in big cities. Here in a village, we hoped to catch a glimpse of a more traditional, pure aspect of Indian culture.

Gene had been growing a beard with little success since he left home and this was the time for the meager harvest. He wanted to shave it off Indian-style and, as if we planned it, we stumbled into the perfect barber shop. Under a tree on the roadside, the village barber was just finishing up with a customer and he welcomed Gene into his chair. I sat down on his cot, ready to enjoy this event and, very quickly, a crowd gathered.

Gene was lathered up and, with a razor-sharp blade, the villager (probably a barber by caste) moved Gene's beard and moustache— one swipe at a time—from his face to a foamy pile on the side of the barber's left hand. The crowd really enjoyed the show. I think the barber got the biggest thrill of all and, after leaving him 2 rupees, Gene walked away with a nice shave.

From Molarband, we rode the bus to the end of the line for 1.5 cents and got off in a commotion of mud-brick huts, outdoor cot beds, wells, muddy white and lazy cows, and curious people. This was Jaitpur. A village that has probably never seen a tourist. Jaitpur had not a hotel, not a restaurant, not a painted house, not a car, not a paved road, and not an English-speaking person anywhere. In other words, it was exactly what we were looking for.

The thing to do in such a village is to walk slowly through it, peering into courtyards, and waving at the people who have stopped

Gene getting a village shave
proved entertaining for all.

Hey! I mean, hay!
Can I lighten your load?

what they're doing to stare and wonder "what are you doing here?" We walked and waved across Jaitpur until we came to the open green fields, and then turned left and worked our way around the fringe of the village. Mostly I felt very foreign, snapping pictures with kind of a guilty feeling until we were invited into a hut.

Getting invited in is just what you hope for when exploring a village, and now we had a chance to get a firsthand look at a village home. Half the village, so bewildered by our presence, followed us in. We accepted but didn't want the chai (tea) they offered. That's always a problem: to be a gracious guest without getting sick on the food and drink you're offered. Tea always looks as dangerous as its setting, but we sipped away. We passed a pack of glucose biscuits around. (Like "Digestive Biscuits," these were a tasty bit of England that was a kind of go to comfort snack for us...so British and well wrapped for cleanliness). Though I was reluctant to accept their food, the village children excitedly tore into ours.

All this time I was trying my best to communicate with the uniformed and dignified man who apparently was our host. We had absolutely no words in common, but we still smiled and babbled away without communication.

After a while, we felt that maybe we were wearing our welcome thin. Besides, sitting on that bed with everyone staring at us was getting kind of old. We excused ourselves and continued our walk through the far reaches of the village.

On the road out of town we came upon four beautiful women carrying huge baskets of grass on their heads. I goofed around with them a bit, discovering that they had a sense of humor, and then I made my move. Crouching under the giant hat of hay, I looked a woman right in the eye. Sharing the shade of all that hay, so suddenly so close together, from opposite worlds yet sharing the same planet, with our noses just inches apart, this will be a vivid memory for each of us. Then, I straightened up, relieving her of her burden.

The load was heavy, but I had so much fun as part of the group transporting what must be cow food down the road. At the intersection, I gave the woman back her grass, she walked one way and we walked the other. It was the kind of moment that makes me choose travel.

After a morning of ladling up memories like this, we were finally saturated and ready to return to the 20th century. We waved down a jeep to catch a short ride back to the paved road.

On the main road we waved down a local bus and crushed our way in. The guidebooks recommend to never venture into these sardine tins on wheels but I think it's a tremendous experience. Muscling our way in and then asking where the bus was heading, I found myself in a crazy tangle of humanity. It was, in a strange way, entertaining. You abandon any sense of "personal space" and everyone just hangs and sits and climbs on everyone else. I stayed in the back and watched the daredevils cling to the doorway at each stop, hoping things would loosen up so they could work their way inside—like corn flakes settles into the box—and the heavy-laden bus sped down the road.

Gene and I had one last stop we needed to make before we returned to Delhi. I felt like I was playing Twister as I weaseled and wormed my way to the front of the bus. At just the right moment, as the bus slowed down, we asked the driver to stop. Gene and I jumped off and the bus rumbled away.

Everything was suddenly peaceful and still. We were in the middle of 700 million Indians...yet also in the middle of nowhere. No bus, no cars, no people, just fields and sky and silence. We both marveled at this remote and totally real corner of India we had reached. We'd be here until the next ride came along.

Our Last Day in Delhi felt a bit pointless... like hanging around the dorm after the last final had been taken. After so much intense sightseeing, we were getting tired—our sleep deficit is taking me from Sleepy to Dopey. Neither of us had much intention of doing much today until our overnight train to Jaipur.

We had a YMCA breakfast ("Corn flex with fried cheaps") while ABBA played on the stereo. Determined to catch up in our journals and write our "missing you more than ever" postcards, we wrote for a while, then played a little "fan baseball," then snoozed.

By noon, we headed out to make the most of our day. I bought a good-looking little Indian history book and Gene picked up a book on Hindu mythology. We had a lunch of omelet, rice, sweet lassi, and 17 "finger chips" (French fries).

We took a rickshaw to the Kinari Bazaar and spent a couple of aimless hours absorbing the intensity of hard labor: hay pounders, paper printers, box makers, steel-pole forgers, and melon squeezers. I got a nice Indian leather watch band from a genuinely nice guy who just made me feel good.

We had discovered that clothes were a real bargain in India and I was getting tired of always wearing my shorts and yellow t-shirt. So I went on a bit of a spree and soon had a whole new outfit—baggy, lightweight drawstring pants, a white "work shirt," and two hand-woven wool vests. I was happy with my new outfit—especially the pouch hanging from my neck rather than pockets. (Still, I wondered if, like so many other souvenirs, my "Indian wardrobe" would just end up in a box back in Seattle...too cool to trash...but totally ignored.)

We found ourselves on literally the bad side of the train tracks amid hungry horses, sacred cows, broken rickshaws, and some pigs so gross we both concluded that they totally deserve their bad reputation. Wallowing in a mountain of rotten melons, treating the bugs like sugar, they rutted happily away.

Back in our room, we were done with the city. We escaped from the crowds. But there's just no escape from this heat and we just laid down on the beds in the middle of our mess and stared at our ceiling fans as they whirled on full speed. We played a few innings of fan baseball.

Leaving our room full of crumpled up paper baseballs, we went downstairs for our last dinner at the YMCA. It was also the finale in our feud, the dining room showdown. Both sides were ready. We took our seats and couldn't get water. Our coffee didn't come until after the meal. And when I poured milk and sugar on my rice and spooned it into the serving bowl, not only our waiter but two of his cohorts sprung to our table and asked the head waiter to do something about us. He tried to smooth things out.

But when we couldn't get any more sugar, Gene brought things to a head. He prowled over to a neighboring table to grab an unused bowl. The waiter could take no more. He confronted Gene, demanding: "How much do you want? Five cubes? A half kilo? One kilo?" It was all so ridiculous, I couldn't help but laugh. It probably was best that this was our last meal here.

After dinner, we rallied a little energy and went down to a movie theater to catch the hottest Indian flick of the season. We paid our 3 rupees each and joined the happy gang of Indian moviegoers. It was entertaining, even though we couldn't understand a word. The love scenes were corny, the fight scenes made the 1960s Batman TV show look realistic, and the musical aspect of the film was really catchy, even beautiful.

*Cinema is huge in India and provides
the traveler with a handy break
from the intensity of the streets.*

When you rent a Maharaja's palace, it comes with three wheels at your beck and call.

This was an "adults only" drama about a beautiful girl who gets her face burned ugly and falls in love with an Indian Frank Sinatra. The sex was totally left up to everyone's imagination, but the kiss and the girl's beautiful-but-clothed body were enough for the censors to classify it "dangerous for those under 18." It was melodramatic enough so that we could follow the Hindi plot without understanding any of the conversation. Sneakily eating our popcorn (it's not allowed inside), we stayed until the finish. The people really get into these films and, for 3 rupees, they get more than their money's worth. So did we.

Just as a wicked monsoon hit, we hopped on a rickshaw and headed through the wind and rain to catch our midnight train. Gene and I were in fantastic spirits as our hair danced down the smiling streets of Delhi. We sang our heads off, waved and joked with passing Indians, and enjoyed our driver's company. We gave him a whopping 5 rupees and it felt good to make him feel good.

The train station was the usual scene of "refugee camp" chaos. Colorful people flickered in the station's beams of light—which created puddles of shining silk and cotton, and caused nose rings, ankle bracelets, and gold teeth to sparkle. Dark eyes followed us as we wandered.

Somewhere along Track 3 we found our car and then Mr. Steves and Mr. Openshaw listed on our 4'10" long "beds." Our berths looked more like empty cupboards. Oh well, this is India, and I accepted it gracefully as I climbed awkwardly into my top bunk, with six pairs of curious eyes following my every move. (Perhaps they were thinking, "This tight fit was the reward we got for the quality nutrition we enjoyed during our growth years.")

I positioned myself, folded jeans padding my tailbone and head on my poncho, and lost myself in my Indian history book. Time flipped by in one-hour snatches, as I laid on one side until sore and then the other…back and forth until the night passed and we were in Jaipur.

Just saying the words "Jaipur" and "Rajasthan" seems to capture the mystique of being in India. I could feel something different right away. Beautiful streets, musty-yet-majestic buildings, but especially the people: colorful, happy, quick with a warm smile, and the women are the most beautiful I've seen in India. The people of Rajasthan also have a fun sense of humor. This place makes me want to get to know more of India and its people.

But first, we needed a place to sleep. Hotel finding is about the hardest work I have to do when traveling, except possibly for writing in this journal. Jaipur was tough. After the Y in Delhi, we wanted a moderate splurge but everything was either not good enough or full. We even accidentally tried a "home for sick people" that I fell in love with from a distance—but I got over that in a hurry when I saw the clientele.

Finally, we came to the Khetri House, where the Maharaja of Khetri stays when he's in Jaipur. It was a stately, if a bit decrepit, old mansion and, at first, we weren't too impressed. Then the quiet courtyard, big garden, huge living room—furnished musty old-English-style, waiting room, big bathroom, abundance of servants, and the peace—the extreme lack of busy-ness, with only tropical birds chirping—grew on us. Gene wavered, but he's always glad after I push a splurge.

We explored our three-room suite and realized that, with the maharaja not in town, we were the total kings of his palace. There

Crazy Baba, with mud caked on his long black hair, jived as he pedaled us through the rain.

Beggars, intentionally deformed
at birth, go to work daily like this.

was no one else here—only me, Gene, and a dozen hired hands to cook our eggs, call the rickshaw, trim the gardens, and offer to do our laundry. We relaxed and then sat down in the lavish, huge, and empty dining room for a big, typical, breakfast. We are really enjoying this fantastic life. It seemed Hindus believed our privileged place in life (or caste) was divinely ordained, which shaped the relationship between servants and elites. As Western tourists...we are off the charts and they just accepted the will of the gods.

Happily settled, we called for a rickshaw, rolled under majestic Chandpole Gate, and entered the old, pink city of Jaipur. As if to welcome us, the sky opened up, and we were washed away in a long, long monsoon downpour. There we sat, drenched, under a skimpy tarp in the only rickshaw in Jaipur without a canopy, while our driver—Crazy Baba—with mud caked on his long black hair, jived as he pedaled us through the rain. On India's bicycle rickshaws, Gene and I just about fit in the tight little two-person seats behind the driver. We've spent literally hours with our hips pressed tightly together, looking at the muscular butts of rickshaw drivers flexing while drenched in a mix of sweat and rain.

Totally wet, we took refuge in a museum of old Mughal paintings, sedan chairs, artifacts, and military equipment—learning about the desert state of Rajasthan while drying out.

When it stopped raining the temperature was actually comfortable, and we spent the rest of the day just enjoying the fascinating pink streets of Jaipur. What a place! Camel trains ambling slowly and carelessly down the main drag; a dark, hairy fat man standing stark naked in his doorway while six monkeys perched on the roof ignore him; bikes, cows, and rickshaws clogging the streets, ladies sitting in a sea of flowers, selling garlands.

Beggars with missing or curly dwarfed limbs clambered down muddy roads, pushing rusty tin cups of coins with their mud-caked heads, while green parrots perched on their sides cackled. (We were told such cripples are intentionally mutilated by their parents in their infancy to be more pathetic and therefore more successful in their caste-determined lives as beggars.) Kids surrounded the hard-to-look-at pairs of scooting beggars, pleading with us to take pictures of the bizarre scene. A man assured us that a crumpled camel lying in the road was just sleeping.

In the market, merchants sold bananas, coconuts, leaf-rolled cigarettes rubber-banded in groups of ten, and sugar cane juice. We stopped in a shop that sold herbs, and the guy whipped out his hashish with a smile and declared it "the ganja of Shiva." We asked him why Shiva—who I knew as "the destroyer" because he destroys ego. He said Shiva is the god of ganja because ganja is one of the five sacred plants, the source of happiness, liberation, and compassion. How could we say no? We gave him 3 rupees (35 cents) for about 5 grams.

I also bought a pair of ankle bracelets. Little by little, I have to make sure I have a gift for everyone at home.

We caught a bus to the Amber Fort. Upon arrival we were pummeled by a terrible downpour. Like everyone else, we took shelter with cows and monkeys under an overhanging eve. In a stunning admission of where they ranked on the animal hierarchy, only the gross pigs went about their muddy business, oblivious to the rain. There we stood, enjoying a world painted and shaped by monsoon streaks and drizzles. Tall, thin people wrapped in tarps splashed by, children were dwarfed by big black umbrellas, the street became a river, and passing cars sprayed a brown wake. I stared at a monkey and he went scampering across the roof and peeked back from the other side. Hanging with the cows, we waited for the rain to let up.

After a while, huge, lumbering elephants appeared on the road below the fortified hilltop. The chance to ride an elephant was exciting, something that for years has been high on my checklist of things

Goin' my way?

to do. I had underlined it in triple in my guidebook, knowing that someday I would come to Jaipur and check this out.

The rain slowed down and Gene and I climbed the little concrete loading tower to "board" our elephant. We paid 5 rupees to take a jaunt through the marketplace on the beast's back, while the driver sat on the elephant's head with a mean-looking spike to steer with. We swayed and rocked high above the traffic and market stalls, holding the umbrellas above us and soaking in this experience with help of the persistent rain. What fun! We took turns riding solo and taking pictures of each other.

Once, as the elephant was coming in for a "landing," I was riding side-saddle and gloriously not paying attention. Then, in a moment of sudden horror, I just got my legs out of the way before the elephant's hide crushed against the concrete. About a second later and my legs would have met a fate much like a worm under my boot.

We were in tremendous spirits (in part because I still had legs), wishing today wasn't over so fast. We bought flower leis to wear on the way home and just lived it up, singing and joking with the people we passed. I knew that Jaipur was a place to come back to.

As darkness fell, we entered the gates of our mansion and walked down the jungle-lined lane that led through the estate to the Khetri House. How jolly good this was. The servants and singing birds greeted us and we were told that "dinner was prepared."

In the dining room, two places out of 30 were set. We sat down and the servants brought on the food. The dinner of mutton, potatoes, pumpkin soup (aka "Indian soup), and banana pudding was fine and the company was funny. When they were done cooking and serving, all the boys from the kitchen gathered around to watch us eat. I suggested that a fifth guy, who wasn't standing there gawking, pull up a chair and join the party. Then a funny "accredited" fortune teller entertained us but failed to draw any money out of us.

Over coffee and pudding, we got into an interesting conversation with the hotel staff covering family planning, castration, Indira Gandhi, political parties, and wives. They don't like Communists, families of more than five kids, China, or castration. They wondered why we hadn't married yet and they insisted we were rich.

After a while, we said goodnight to the servants we share with the Maharaja of Khetri and went up to our suite. We sent Lord Shiva some smoke signals and took a very interesting walk in the dark garden. Suddenly, the shadows and distant voices swirled in the cool, star-filled breeze. Then, we simply sat on the royal porch of the Maharaja and looked out.

If there's one must-see sight in India, it's the one we're heading for today. After one last service-heavy breakfast, we loaded up our bags and checked out. Waving goodbye to our friends at the Maharaja's palace and all that musty splendor, we passed through the great pink stone gate one last time and hailed a rickshaw to the bus station. If you ever wonder where the Hippie Trail tourists are going, just look for the brightly colored backpacks in the sea of dirty canvas brown bags at the bus station. And it was clear here: all were Agra-bound...ready for the Taj Mahal.

Once in Agra, we signed up for a city tour and boarded the "ordinary bus." The "deluxe bus" was air-conditioned, included cold drinks, cost twice as much, and was filled with Westerners. Our tour was mostly Indians from Delhi as eager to see the Taj Mahal as we were. (As India is about like Europe when it comes to having lots

Another view of the Taj Mahal

of languages, they need one common language for tourism. And, thanks to their British colonial heritage, that language is mine so our tour was in English.)

First, we drove out of town to a deserted palace city called Fatehpur Sikri that Emperor Akbar had built. It took years and millions of man hours to build, and Akbar abandoned it shortly after moving in for lack of water. That left an eerie, impressive ghost town that, 400 years later, tourists would wander through, being chased by hawkers and beggars. It was huge and beautiful! Nice Mughal architecture by any standards. We saw the harem, the patio-sized parcheesi board that used sexy maidens for pieces, and a huge complex of royal buildings, all out in the middle of Indian nowhere.

After touring the big mosque, I passed time, as one does when waiting for a bus to depart, by bargaining with the aggressive merchants out my window. Show interest (just a glance) and you'll weather a barrage of things for sale: rattles, wooden snakes, faded postcards, bananas, peacock fans, and jewelry. As the bus began to roll, the merchants actually run with it, still trying to close a deal.

We rolled on to the big Agra Fort. This red fort was built in 1565 by Akbar, the grandfather of Shah Jahan who built the Taj Mahal. We toured it, getting a great view of the Taj just down the Yamuna River, and seeing many of the lavish buildings housed inside its two-mile long and 70-foot-high wall. Gardens, well-watered plants, the river, and a cool fresh breeze made the fort a pleasant place for an afternoon visit.

The last part of our tour, and a highlight for sure, was the famous Taj Mahal. This marble tomb was built from 1631 to 1653 by 20,000 laborers for one lady, Mumtaz Mahal. She was the wife and love of Shah Jahan, the fourth Mughal ruler since Babur, and apparently quite a guy.

We were free to roam and soak in its beauty. I was blown away by the gentle harmony of the beautiful marble dome, minarets, gardens, and ponds. This was probably number one on my list of things to see and now it's right up there with the Kremlin and Versailles on my list of favorite sights of all time.

I thought for years that it would probably be smaller than I imagined, dusty, cramped by neighboring buildings, surrounded by an unkempt, burned-off garden, cluttered with beggars, hawkers, animals, and swarming with tourists, sweating under a merciless sun. It was absolutely none of that. It was simply majestic, and more beautiful than any postcard or picture could ever be.

The Taj is not something to be rushed. You must stand there and let your eyes play up and down its graceful yet strong lines. The inside was nothing special—just a couple of modest tombs under an everyday dome—but from the outside the Taj Mahal is everything. We let the tour go on without us and lingered, watching the setting sun shape the lines and shadows and warm up the white of the marble surfaces. We walked around the lush gardens, catching it from different angles. The clouds got dark and heavy leaving just a light stripe on the horizon and raindrops obliterated the reflections in the pond. We gazed through the gate at that great white monument of love…it was silent, pristine, and all ours.

We finished our visit with a cold drink, then sat on the grass, with chipmunks and red horizons, and just soaked it in. The lovely Taj Mahal.

At the Taj Mahal in Agra

On the streets of Varanasi

Like Hindu pilgrims, we were Varanasi bound. By 6:30 we had found the seats labeled Openshaw and Steves and we rattled away from Agra on the overnight train to Varanasi. Second class ain't bad if reserved seats are required. Then you know there will be only one person per seat and no sorry soul sprawled out under your seat. The seats were hard and the windows were barred but we were rolling in the right direction and the stars were out.

I managed to lose myself in our old but unread *Time* magazine. On the road, old news is still news if you've yet to read it. Peanut shells were everywhere, some bugs had found my juicy body, and every once in a while, a sad-looking beggar would wail by and everyone would totally ignore the poor wretch.

I was as comfortable as could be expected. Plus I was enjoying my breezy new white pants and the pouch I wore around my neck as a substitute for pockets.

To pass some time, I did exercises in my "lern-to-spell" book and we played a little trip trivia. Then we made up our bunks, spreading a little padding in crucial spots on the hard wood, and tried to go to sleep. We felt like luggage stretched out where, on a European train, you'd find peoples' bags.

The night was as long as the bed was hard. I couldn't stretch out and passed the time grabbing several one-hour snatches of sleep. At 5 a.m. or so, I called it quits. I twisted around and gazed out the open door, marveling at how beautiful India was as its green fields, sleepy villages, and monsoon floods rolled by. At each stop a parade of sellers, beggars, deformed people, and various hawkers would march or crawl by. I bought a vicious-looking knife from a guy for 5 rupees and gave a beggar lady a coin.

At 8:00, we pulled into the holy city of Varanasi. As usual, scores of "helpful" hustlers were waiting like baby birds for their mothers' worms. Nobody was getting my worm and we marched through the mob and hopped on a rickshaw to find our own hotel. We splurged for a nice, big, clean, air-conditioned room, with a complete bathroom and breakfast, for 75 rupees (about $9.50). I love checking in to a hotel early enough to enjoy breakfast the day of your arrival… and that's what we did.

❋　❋　❋

Varanasi is a bustling, thrown-together old town, the holiest and most full of pilgrims in India. The streets are clogged with thin, nearly naked people, bicycles, rickshaws, cows, and rarely a motor-driven vehicle, except for huge, WWII-vintage buses filled with pilgrims. It looked like it would be hard to rise above this squalor without resorting to a very expensive hotel. While we hoped for something just clean, basic and comfortable, because we needed a refuge, we ended up with extravagant, got a place with air conditioning, and now, as I write, I'm sitting happily in front of that wonderful machine. Cool.

We were in a market area and spent a couple hours walking and browsing. We found ourselves in a car-free traffic jam, a crazy tangle of humans and bikes. The road was simply clogged to a standstill by people. Later we ventured into an industrial area, where dozens of boys and men pounded silver into paper-thin sheets for 12 hours a day. Beyond them toiled lock-makers, blacksmiths, and woodworkers.

We caught a rickshaw to the bazaar. It's really bad when your rickshaw driver doesn't know where he's going and pretends like he does.

Pilgrims and backpackers alike converge on the holy city of Varanasi on the holy river Ganges.

We finally just said stop. I gave him 2 rupees and he looked at me with a well-practiced look of astonishment and said "6." I told him he was crazy, put the 2 rupees on his knee, and walked off. The basic rule is if you don't draw complaints when you pay someone, you're overpaying.

Every tourist in this city is harried from dawn till dusk by people of all kinds who see each tourist as a walking money tree. Harvest season lasts all year and the ultimate prize is the rich American. Every rickshaw man, hotel worker, and riverboat boy seems to have a sitar teacher who knows Ravi Shankar and would love to play for us, a friend who will sell us silk for less than cost, a great little market for us to check out, and lots of other fantasies.

We found the bazaar just as the monsoon did and we jumped from the cover of one colorful and dripping shop to the next, splashing through a world of trinkets, blazing reds, elegant saris, and monsoon rain.

One smooth-talking rickshaw driver took us to hear sitar and tabla music. Shoes off and waiting for the inevitable sales pitch, we watched as two stylish-looking musicians warmed up and worked into a morning raga with a 16-beat tala. We didn't really know what was expected of us, so we just sat and enjoyed and learned, as they were happy to entertain questions between ragas. Music with no Western-style meter or mode—actually enjoying something I thought I knew but didn't—was freeing.

Then we decided to take a bus tour to see Varanasi's main sights. We stood around with ten other tourists waiting for the bus to arrive, surrounded by hungry rickshaw drivers very willing to act as the buses' substitutes. One hour and a great dancing monkey show later, the bus came.

Our friendly guide enthusiastically showed a temple overrun with spoiled monkeys—so privileged in Hindustan. I'd heard how monkeys were expert at stealing glasses. They seemed to eye me devilishly as I nervously hung on to my glasses.

The Maharaja's Fort gave us a look at the lifestyle of the Maharajas during British rule: the elephant costumes, sedan chairs, and bizarre weapons. And then we even got a look at a real-life Maharaja. The silly little band played horribly and a dilapidated circa-1955 car stood waiting as the word spread that the Maharaja was coming. All of us tourists readied our cameras and then he came. This short man in a rumpled suit was a living "dead" institution. His fort was a shambles, his band was embarrassing, and power and glory belonged only to his ancestors. I'm surprised his car started.

Then the monsoon opened up in full fury, and we fled into the bus. After a quick look at the Ganges, the tour was over and the bus took us home.

❊   ❊   ❊

Today we were up at 4:30 a.m. joining the other pilgrims to visit the Ganges River.

We started so early because sunrise is the hour of intense worship and rituals along the banks of the holy Ganga (Ganges) River. Every Hindu should make a pilgrimage at least once to this holy site. This is the best place to die, and thousands of old Hindus spend their last years here, waiting to do just that. Then it is traditional to be cremated and have your ashes thrown into this sacred river.

It was still dark as we motorscooter-rickshawed through town. The sun was warming the horizon and we wanted to be on the river for its first appearance. People were flocking to the river and, as the sun rose, bells rang and the religious activity intensified.

After warnings about beggars, hawkers, and pickpockets, we marched single file, with a protective hand on our cameras and our heads high, trying to look above the misery and filth that carpeted the narrow alleyway we were following down to the sacred Ganga.

Along the way, hawkers tried desperately to sell their wares at ridiculously low prices. Beggars looked as weak and miserable as

The maharaja still had his palace,
his guard, and his limo—but it was
all pretty comically run down.

Devout Hindus from across India make
pilgrimages to the sacred waters of
the Ganges.

possible, many showing rotten skin, scabs, or sores that were just swarming with bugs. Some people just sat motionless, head down, with a small pile of rice on their lap, hoping for more. Others held lifeless babies. And some just ignored the world, pursuing good karma.

We got to the milky shore of the Ganges and rustic old boats were waiting. We found one and slowly worked our way upstream. We had cameras poised to take home images of this intense religious happening, rituals that seems so strange to we Western Christians. It was nice to have our own boat, and our guide was actually helpful. We came to the *ghats,* or stairs, which today, because of the monsoon rains, were mostly under the swollen waters of the Ganges.

We stopped at one special *ghat* and quietly observed the action. People drink the water, jump into it, wash in it, do all kinds of rituals in it, or just sit prayerfully in it. We saw holy men walking down to the steps, where they waited as various pilgrims kissed their feet. We almost overdosed on the total experience: shriveled bodies clad in scanty rags, clinging to brass spittoon-like jars full of Ganges water; ladies dressed up in rich silk saris, taking sacred sips pensively in the swirling current; dark men wearing barely more than a penis-sheath, dropping flower petals; and women with pancake breasts, who were beyond caring about dumb things like covering your body.

These people seemed at peace and thankful to be cleansing their bodies and souls in the filthy but supposedly healing water. Many had traveled across India for this bath. Many would never leave during this life. If they died here and had their ashes thrown into the river, they would escape the drudgery of reincarnation. They would rise above all that, reaching Nirvana, a kind of oneness with God, freeing oneself of individuality and egoism. They all seemed very fulfilled, happy…and not afraid of death.

I felt a bit rude treating their religious acts like an exhibit or a trip to the zoo (Gene put it well—"philistine"), but I was still excited to witness this firsthand, and the bathers didn't seem to care about the wide-eyed, camera-toting tourists that filed by.

Then we came to the dramatic climax of our morning tour: the place where bodies were cremated on open fires. We all knew it was here somewhere, but only after spotting the columns of black smoke did we know where. We actually got out of the boats and walked up to a viewpoint to see the bodies disappearing into the holy fires. Attendants kept things orderly as blackened feet, like logs on a fire, crumpled slowly into the flames. Setting my exposure and shutter speed in advance, I snapped a picture. Even though I was quick, I was spotted...and had to exit early with some angry Indians on my tail.

With that, we were ready to leave this incredible river and head into town. This was our chance to prowl aimlessly and really saturate our senses with all the intensities of a Hindu's life along the Ganges. We stopped by a golden temple and walked several powerful blocks through India at its grisliest, most shocking and, at the same time, richest. All kinds of flies and bugs adorned all kinds of crap that filled one kind of alley: dirty alleys leading to the riverfront. In one empty alley we turn a corner and find ourselves face to face with a giant but meek cow.

There's a lot of squalor and heartache here, but there's also a lot of joy. I find I'm able to think of India in terms of bulk joy rather than joy per person, and perhaps that's why I see it as such a rich and wondrous place.

Fragrant breezes, tranced music, quivering flames, painted bodies, and cremations that mean the world to some and nearly nothing to others...it's all part of a visit to the milky Ganges.

*Travelers in small boats floated
by the steps to observe faithful
Hindus worshipping.*

The back streets of Varanasi—
the home of Lord Shiva and about
two thousand temples—were intense.

We ate our last breakfast in India to the pummeling rhythm of the pouring monsoon. The hot milk made my Corn Flex instantly mush. We hailed a rickshaw which muscled us through the center of old Varanasi and to the north side of town. There we stood, in the drizzle, trying to flag down a ride to Nepal.

I felt awkward hitching Indian-style, which isn't sticking out your thumb but waving your hand in a downward motion. But it worked and after a few minutes, a big truck stopped and the Sikh at the wheel said he was going to north and welcomed us into his cab. I thought it would be too crowded. But we managed to fit five men and our two rucksacks into the front seat (I sat between the driver and his door) and we were on our way.

In India, so much is "makeshift," broken but working smoothly through what my Dad taught me was "field expediency" and this truck was no exception. The starter was a loose wire, the window on one side was just a hole plugged by a plastic pillow, a random bolt kept the glove compartment shut, and colorful pictures of Hindu gods decorated the cab, keeping us out of the ditch.

We rambled along at 30 miles per hour and we were 120 miles out of Gorakhpur. The rain came down as we rolled steadily past floods, hordes of vultures, camels both grazing and hauling, women decorating brown wells with rainbows of laundry, and overturned trucks—there were lots of accidents.

When we stopped for a break, the trucker gave us tea and we

shared our glucose biscuits. Then we spotted a bus just down the road that was also northern-bound. We decided (just for a new experience and a change of scene) to say thank you and *namaste* to our truck friends and pile into the bus.

For a while, the bus just sat there, and the Sikh truck driver's parting words of "We will arrive before you" rang in my ears. But once every seat was full and we took off, this bus flew—no stops, no animals, not even anyone standing in the aisle. The kilometers ticked away as we splashed through rivers rushing over the road. Wet, tired, and hungry, we'd made it to our final destination in India, the last stop before Nepal—Gorakhpur.

Our wheels hit Gorakhpur with a splash, and we stepped out of our bus into a wicked downpour, finding ourselves in a strange wilderness bus station. Around us was dripping jungle. It looked as if it had been raining nonstop for a hundred years.

We took a scooter for a joyride through the swamped town, laughing at our crazy situation. We were stuffed into this tiny three-wheeler, forcibly reclined in the broken back seat with two other people, rain drooling all over the place, and the driver's pink plastic tarp flapping in our faces doing more to sprinkle water than to shield us from it.

I was actually enjoying this monsoon-India. It's so warm that the wetness is just wetness and this is undeniably a big part of life in India. The deluge wettens the collective smile of this land. These people live with this intense rainfall, happily, for a good chunk of every year. The monsoon is water. And water is life.

We returned to the bus station only to find that the next bus to the Nepal border may or may not run today.

Now it struck me—I was deep in India. The big cities were India, but western and tame. Here I was in a small town bus station and there was no English script anywhere—not even our numbers. Everything was in totally foreign Hindi. People squatted around in

*With the monsoon came flooding.
Hitching a ride on a big truck, we
found that fording raging rivers
seemed routine to our driver.*

groups, painted, draped, wet, and not caring. Then two guys in white robes walked in with long vicious spears! Wow! I had to go over and check that out! Spears!

Buses routinely came and went late, as if time has no value. It occurred to me that when I'm most frustrated by India, it's because of what I consider a disrespect for the value of time. I treat time like money…I even talk about it like money: I spend it, save it, waste it, and invest it. But in India, time is like bubble gum…it's a mix of worthless and forever. You just fiddle with it. You have to spend 24 hours somehow to live a day and this way was as good as any.

With no bus to the border in sight, we joined some Indian travelers in renting a jeep, for 10 rupees each. Like backpacking birds, we chirped "cheap Jeep," and climbed in. There were seven people packed in for the two-hour ride. I sat in front with the driver and a new Indian friend, and Gene had to pack into the back with five others. There are no tourists here, only travelers. With drips dropping everywhere and puddles exploding out from under the Jeep, we headed north, hoping the roads were still navigable. "Cheap Jeep!"

What a ride. I was in the highest of spirits as we zig-zagged madly through the holy cows, drenched passing bicyclists, and bounced to the rhythm of the blaring Indian movie music as everyone on board sang along. I couldn't tell if the bodies of water that stretched sometimes for miles on either side of the road were lakes or floods. I suspect these "lakes" were seasonal.

After a tea stop and lots of "Glucose Biscuits" we came to the India-Nepal border. It was, as might be expected, strange. The office was a desk in a tea shop with a laid-back, friendly bureaucrat who slowly and routinely stamped passports. We met a Peace Corps volunteer who had served two years in Nepal, and he was a godsend to talk to. He had grown to love the country, its mountains, its wilderness, its tempo of life, and especially its people, who he called "sweet." When I asked him about health, he was nonchalant. "Oh,

I've been pretty good really. I haven't had dysentery for quite a while. I've got worms though." (They say along the Hippie Trail there are two kinds of travelers: "those who know they have worms and those who don't.")

Worms. Well—I guess I'll be careful while I'm here and drag any worms out before they get all the way in. This morning Gene and I took the first of our supposedly "miracle pills" which we've been saving for the home stretch of our trek. Brand new, and at a dollar apiece, hopefully they'll protect us from any miscellaneous bugs. Or worms.

Customs was a breeze, and we changed money—1,195 Nepali rupees for $50, and I expect things will only cost two-thirds as much here as in India.

Ooo, I was thrilled to be here. And there's something particularly right about crossing a country overland rather than flying effortlessly into its major city. So, through the puddles we splashed, and under the happy arch that read: "Welcome to Nepal."

We had to spend all of our money without running
out. This took some planning but was quite [...]
For our 3rd night in a row we [...]
for dinner and they let us [...]
Three french fries with [...]
pork in the sweet [...]
This to the [...]
rectified [...]
Quit[...]
ever[...]

I really don't trust my watch. And I don't trust our
hotel's wake up service but we managed to get up
and out of our hotel by just after 7:00. A raggy
[i]ble of a marching band did its morning jaunt
[ ] the square and we went down to the
[ ] for a fancy last breakfast. We had
[ ] roysees before we left so
[ ] I enjoyed a cheese
[ ] porridge.
[ ] [ ]ved yesterday.
[ ] [ ]ve had

Nepal

August 28
September 4

Arriving in Nepal, 1978

From nuclear power to flower power, from mighty to fragrant, from bad roads to dirt roads, right away I knew this place was different. Everyone smiled and had a sense of humor—rickshaw bikers, customs officials, and little poor kids splashing playfully in the mud. This was one of the poorest countries in the world, with a per capita income of just over $100 a year. This is a country that *India* gives aid to. This is a place that makes *India* look advanced. But this is a proud, peaceful, and as far as I can tell, happy land. I'm so glad to be in Nepal.

Piling onto a minibus, we rode for four cents into the first town across the border.

What an eye-opening ride! I clung to a corner of a bench and just gawked at the people around me. The Nepalis looked more Tibetan or Mongolian. The lady in front of me was beautifully adorned— deep blue-and-red sari, a large brass ring shining from her nose, tattooed hands, and seven holes in each ear—four gold earrings and three empty holes including one large enough to see through. The bracelets covering her forearm and the healthy twinkle in her eyes made her quite an impressive sight. Unlike my impression of Indian women, she was independent and in control enough to look me right in the eye. For lack of an alternative form of communication, she smiled. Across from her, an old man carefully fingered a pile of coins in his hand that couldn't have amounted to more than 5 cents. Then, next to me, a fat girl wrapped in red silk leaned over her smiling husband and retched out the window, making a very miserable face and then regaining her composure as if nothing happened. Worms…

We switched buses at a crossroads lined with nothing but woven roofed shelters housing pineapples and coconuts for sale.

This was a friendly bus. Buddhists, curious women, happy fat men, and four goats—three black and one white. I shared my front bench with the shaved Buddhist and the three black goats. I struck up a conversation with a delightful man who had served in the British army but liked the quiet Nepal countryside better. He warmed me all over just by talking with me. He said he couldn't visit me in America but he would see me in paradise. With a heartfelt handshake and a great belly laugh, he stepped off the bus and out of my life. (I'm learning the world is filled with such people.) I offered my treasured Glucose biscuits to everyone around me and, predictably, no one accepted. (To be honest, that was both my hope and expectation.) Gene and I munched as we approached the exciting first hills of the Himalayas that vanished into the heavy monsoon clouds.

We made a rest stop in Butwal—the last town on the Indian plain—which butted right up against the Himalayan wall. Butwal was exciting. Not much really, but this was Nepal and being in a new culture, simple things take on a fresh appeal. Boys balancing baskets of chickens on a pole, the new brands of bottled soft drinks of questionable cleanliness, a strange mix of local clothing with loud bell bottoms and Western t-shirts. Men sitting tightly cross-legged under the shelter of their bicycle rickshaws, and pigs rolling in the sputtering-in-the-rain mud. A frog dashed in front of me as we ran to our bus, just catching it as it pulled out. Taking our seats, we were joined by the same four goats, and we rolled out of Butwal.

Quickly becoming lost in the heavily vegetated mountains, we rose high above the plain. I was glad we took this slow local bus. I couldn't imagine a better "welcome to Nepal" tourist activity. Everything was perfect. I hung my head out the window and drank

Leaving the "Hotel Shiddartha for Homely" ... "Please Get Here." Tansen, Nepal

in the lush green, thrilling cliffs, swollen rivers, dreamy waterfalls, green-carpeted terraces, and tropical-looking villages complete with bright-eyed mothers running out with their babies and pointing to the foreigner who was passing through. Long, frail, suspension footbridges stretched across gorges, and Gene and I were tickled as could be. Suddenly, Gene grimaced in pain. I didn't know what was happening. Then, through clenched teeth, he said, "That goat is stepping on my foot!"

We climbed for about an hour, and just as darkness set in, we came to our destination: a tiny village perched right on the top of a ridge—lovely Tansen.

This place was great—totally unspoiled! I can hardly wait to see it in the morning light. We were relieved to find it had electricity, and it hit us—this was the first time that the existence of electricity has ever been a concern. We have really escaped it all.

Stepping over the goats, we got out and found a hotel right on the main square for 16 rupees. It was surprisingly nice with screens on the windows, a clean-looking restaurant, and even canopied beds. The sign outside said it all: "For homely. Please get here."

I was writing away in this journal, nearly finished with today's long entry, when Gene came running in, excited.

There was a religious ceremony in the streets. The procession—which would go on for a few hours—was the first anniversary of a Tansen man's death.

We ran through the dark alleys and caught up with the mysterious parade: twenty young men in dress-up white outfits and four with green leis or necklaces were holding hands and singing the same song over and over. Moving slowly down the street, they were surrounded by half of the village, drawing people to every window and illuminated by six men wearing kerosene lanterns like hats. Two sparkling and painted women, looking like princesses or goddesses, followed silently under a brightly colored umbrella, and behind everyone were the drummer and harmonium player carrying their instruments with straps across their foreheads. Making a commotion in the background was the town fool, very drunk and obnoxious, and a few brawling dogs.

Following this magical procession, we wandered through a timeless village floating in a wonder-world. The full moon lit the endlessly layered valley and between each row of hills, a white pillow of clouds cuddled.

Climbing deeper into the ancient kingdom of Nepal, my spirit soared. Our bus from Tansen to Pokhara wound through the lush mountains, braving rockslides and nearly washed-out roads. At one point, one guy got out and ran down the one-lane "highway," tossing fallen stones out of the way.

As our rusty old bus clung to the tenuous edge, I hung my head out the window, looking straight down at a vigorous river, long and lonely rope footbridges, thatched huts, and green, dripping terraces. (Slow bus rides with open windows big enough to feel the wind while literally leaning into the views are my favorites.)

We passed through several small towns and villages. Most were no more than a row of huts along the roadside. Until recently, when this road was built, this region was accessible only by air or trail. Western t-shirts and Eveready batteries have now found their way in, but I don't think a lot has changed here. The villagers still squat, wide-eyed, as the buses pass through. I haven't seen a single other Westerner since the Nepal border.

The kilometers passed slowly. I thought of a book I enjoyed—

Pedaling to the Seti River

Man with prayer wheels in Nepal

Reflections on the Basic Causes of Human Misery—that made the case that some of Earth's happiest people were happy because they lived on land poor in natural resources and difficult to live on…land that no other group of people wanted. Perhaps this is why the Nepali expression, when at rest, seems to be a gentle smile.

As we entered the Pokhara Valley, blue sky began beating the clouds away. The bus became very crowded…painfully crowded. A powerful Nepali woman wedged herself so strongly onto my bench I was nearly hanging from the window. Just as my body started to scream, we pulled into the bus station of Nepal's second-largest city—Pokhara. Staggering out, I found myself in another one of those Asian cities that are missing a skyline. Since land is so plentiful, they just sprawl everywhere.

Our first task was to set up in a hotel. In a far-out place like this you seek out the tourist area (the kind of zone you try to avoid in Europe) and we began walking to where the hotels clustered. Distances were greater than we thought, and we walked and walked. I must be getting soft in my old age because all the cheap hotels turned me off and we searched on for something a bit more comfortable. I guess money corrupts and softens. I've got more of it now than I used to, and it really stretches here in Nepal. We needed order and cleanliness. And we found it at the Hotel Mount Annapurna.

This was posh, and we were impressed. For $5 each we got a great corner room right on the mountain side. The dining room was decorated Tibetan, the service and setting was royal, and the food safe and good. Everything was just right, including a private solid-stone bath and Western toilet with a view of the Himalayas. We kicked off our shoes, turned on the fan, and plopped on the beds.

As I sit here at my desk, barefoot and not even worrying about bugs, I decided that the more far away and exciting the place you're visiting, the more value there is in having a nice hotel.

✳   ✳   ✳

Nepal

I am determined to use every bit of the limited time I have in Nepal to its fullest. We set out on rental bikes—past the scenic lake, past the king's palace. We came to Devi's Falls, a tiny gorge with a hole to nowhere that a gushing river thunders through and into. Framed in mist and a rainbow, we watched as the once-peaceful river twisted violently and plummeted out of sight. I didn't know a raging river could just suddenly disappear into the earth like that.

We pedaled into "downtown" Pokhara, the central business district. We parked our bikes and just strolled around. What an enjoyable little place. I think I'm in one of the world's most beautiful corners. People, chickens, cows, water buffalo, and dogs filled the street and there wasn't another tourist to be found. We took an interesting walk down a long side street and, with zoom lens poised, I found lots of great shots.

We came to Pokhara's "freak street," named for the "Hippie freaks" that gathered there. It seems each city along the Hippie Trail from Istanbul to Kathmandu has its freak street, the place where the hip-set of long-term young, very on-the-cheap travelers hang out, wear local clothes and jewelry, smoke a lot of dope, and treat time like bubble gum.

We visited Pokhara's bread factory—wonderfully primitive mass production—and bought four big rolls. They were piping hot, just out of the oven, and painted with melted butter. Humble hand painted signs with slogans like "Go gay with cold drinks!" hawked whatever was for sale. We went gay and bought two very cold bottles of the local pop. With our first sip, we gave up on our self-imposed rule of not drinking locally bottled drinks.

The shops were fantastic. I went a little wild. My rate of consumption is directly correlated to my mood and I was in a buying mood. Gene and I discovered some great 1979 Buddhist and Hindu calendars with wild pictures on them—great for gifts. Up the street, I fancied a rustic teapot and asked, *"Kati paisa?"* (How

I bought this kettle for 15 rupees.

The woman who sold me this dapper
Nepali hat said it looked great on me...

much money?) The guy weighed it and told me 15 rupees. I got it, plus four metal cups and two primitive wooden combs. I'm starting to think about outfitting an apartment when I get home—it's fun. I said, *"dhan'yavāda"* (thank you) and *namaste* (aloha), making the traditional prayer sign with my hands, and left to explore further.

I bought one of the jaunty Nepali hats that all the men wear. I felt like I was wearing a striped tea cozy. Gene said it looked like an "Archie and Jughead" hat. But the giggly Nepali girls who gathered around thought it looked cute…I like to think that's why they were laughing.

We pedaled off through town. The biking was hard work but we were well rewarded. I got a push up a hill from a little kid on his bike and we coasted past a peopled *peepal* tree.

Pokhara is blessed with giant *peepal* trees—what I mistakenly thought was called a "people tree." These shady fig trees are often ringed by concrete benches, and provide a great, cool place for people to sit and "take a rest" like the sign on the tree says. Even the airstrip uses one as its waiting room.

On the roadside through town, some Tibetan refugee craftsmen were waiting with their intriguing goods spread out before them: pounded metal mugs, Buddhist prayer wheels, yak carpets, Chinese cutlery sets (knife and chopsticks) to be hung at your waist, and bells with ethereal resonance. One old guy looked like he'd been wandering the Tibetan highlands for 60 years. We sat down on the grass and slowly he laid all his merchandise out between us. I didn't see a thing I liked until he carefully unwrapped a Buddhist lama drum. What a curious little drum. Wondering what in the world would I do with it, I picked it up for 20 rupees.

These Tibetan handicrafts were so exotic that we pedaled on to their source—the Tibetan refugee camp. Here we were greeted with happy cries, and people came rushing from all corners to sell us their stuff. One lady, with a smiley mouth full of gold and a baby hanging from her saggy breast, held out all kinds of silver bracelets and rings. It was a delightful scene.

First, we entered the rug-weaving industrial shed and the air was filled by a religious-sounding work chant that all the cross-legged, hard-working women were murmuring. It was strange to see the tedious work mixed up with the circular pattern of the music. Babies, as if calmed by the song, stared out the windows and mothers hammered and wove. Slowly, very slowly, Tibetan carpets of beautiful designs took shape. In the next building we followed the raw wool down its course, becoming heavy yarn ready to be made into carpet.

We sat in the little tea shop and reviewed the wares, both old and new, showing interest when we wanted to begin a round of bargaining. After a lot of hard bargaining, I came away with a great silver bracelet, a Tibetan ring, and a rugged looking "dragon" bracelet. Then I aimed for something more substantial: some heavy, rustic metal cups. They offered 90 rupees each, I offered 100 for the three best cups, and that drew laughter—my first offer always does. In the end I walked away with the second and third best cups for 30 rupees each. Those will be great back in Seattle.

With a goodbye that was echoed 20 or 30 times, Gene and I pedaled down the grassy road back to the main drag. We came to the end of the road and to the cave. A talkative man with a big flashlight took us hundreds of feet deep into the cool, dark, and dripping cave for a nice little tour. We pedaled on, eventually stopping at a grassy cliff with a commanding view. With mountains stretching across the gorgeous Seti River winding below us, we savored the moment. We just sat on the edge watching water buffalo ford the river and both thinking about where we were, from a "step back and be thankful" perspective.

With the sun low, our spirits high, and our legs tired, we pedaled on to Phewa Lake. In the shadow of Buddha's temple, ten long-haired freaks sat wrapped in a towel or sun-bleached underwear, staring out over the lake, a white trail of smoke snaking above them to the tune of a bluesy harmonica.

Smoking hash is cheap and easy here and enjoying it seems almost like a tourist cliché, like drinking beer in Germany or tea and scones in England. We bought a pineapple, a melon, a lemon, and a couple grams of hash (all for around a dollar) and returned to our hotel. The valet parked and locked our bikes for us and we went upstairs, got out the pipe, and made a fruit salad to be remembered.

"Ringworm," the beloved mink I bought in Herat (who I now call Herr Rat), was getting moist and smelly. So, every day I tie him to the ceiling fan and whip him around for a few minutes. Today he's much better: smelling less and getting some of that old Herr Rat gleam back in his hair. Then I took a great shower. Just to lie under the whirling fan naked and dripping wet felt so good.

After another smoke, we went downstairs for a funny dinner. I was really living. It was almost silly to consider the prices on the menu—everything was so cheap. We enjoyed chicken curry and *momos* (dumplings) with water buffalo meat. (We nicknamed the meat "tough buff." Rather than actually swallow it, we'd chew all the nutritional value out of it until a tight little wad of gristle remained, which we'd place daintily on the side of our dinner plate.)

Gene and I were both eating well, healthy and happy, and we lingered over a second pot of coffee, just relaxing. It was great to have healthy Gene back. Afterward, we went up on the rooftop to survey the moonlit town of Pokhara and "sense" as much as we could. Drums and singing…fortissimo crickets…sailing clouds. And I knew the invisible Himalayas lurked powerfully above it all. We both agreed, having come here overland all the way from Istanbul… having earned it—made moments like this even sweeter.

Phewa Lake, near Pokhara, Nepal

Phewa Lake by canoe was high on our list. The monsoon thunder, lightning, and wild rain woke us at 4:30 and we knew there'd be no sunrise on the mountains. We've been hoping the clouds would part to reveal the Himalayas they'd been hiding ever since our arrival in Nepal. It wasn't until after breakfast that the weather cleared and, while those clouds still clung persistently to the mountains, we knew we were in for another hot and sunny day.

We pedaled out to Phewa Lake. It blesses this valley in a way that has you thinking "what is a valley without a lake?" Nepalis fished, tourists paddled dugout canoes around the lake and, at the little island-like temple sticking out on a peninsula, the hip tourists who inhabit these parts for months at a time lazed under mothering trees, strumming guitars and each other's hair and, of course, smoked the local ganja.

I have never ridden in a dugout canoe and now was my chance. We hired a long, black dugout. Light, fast, and tippy, it was a fun experience...especially with a little help from Shiva's favorite weed.

Then Gene and I clumsily paddled out to the middle of the lake, where we let her drift while we swam from the boat. This was a fine way to spend the afternoon. I simulated "man overboard" falls and goofed around until we decided to eat our little box of Glucose Biscuits. Just then clouds hid the sun and, dripping wet, I actually felt cold—a wonderful feeling these days.

We found ourselves drifting to the far side of the lake and into sight came a dreamy little bay lined with old dugouts and rice paddies

*Nepal is so poor, India gives
it aid. And a water pump is
a gift that gives and gives.*

and bounded by jungle with a waterfall on one side and a village thatched to a hill on the other. Wow!

We would be fools not to check this scene out. Our first desire was to climb to that inviting waterfall. We beached our boat, were greeted with *namastes* by a couple of the local kids, and found the trail that would take us from the beach, through the jungle, and, hopefully, up to the falls.

After 30 or 40 yards we realized this would not be easy. Not only was it more overgrown, the trail was thickly infested with wild and horrifying insects. Some flew and others moved very fast but the one that had us shaking was the nightmarish Nepali leech. Yuck! The thought of some gross, slimy jungle thing sucking my blood was terrible—even rivaling the thought of a hookworm crawling up into my feet, laying eggs, and eventually raising a thriving family in my stomach. Neither of us wanted to trailblaze past the leeches and through the gummy spiderwebs.

But the draw of the tropical waterfall kept us going. We ditched the kids and kept climbing. On the way, we came upon a long, frantically busy line of ants, really moving along in a fast but orderly single file. I placed a small rock in their path and was fascinated by the confusion that followed, and how a messenger would always be sent back to effectively reestablish communications and set the stupid "follower" ants back on course.

Then, while we were resting and just hanging around on a rock, it came: The Leech…slowly and confidently working its wormy way toward our flesh. I'm sure it could almost taste our blood. Like a heat-seeking slinky, it came slow and steady. Rhythmically, head over tail, it marched as only a leech can toward our pink and uncalloused flesh. We'd stand boldly, luring it toward us, taunting it, and then…at the last moment…we'd take a step away. The leech, undeterred, trudged on. It was strangely thrilling. Finally, we moved on, though we remained on guard. I was glad leeches don't fly.

I wasn't sure we'd make it to our waterfall until we found a high trail that took us there directly. It was like a fantasy version of a tropical waterfall, it reminded me of an Herbal Essence shampoo commercial. We just had to shower under the beautiful cascade. Even with the sun behind clouds and the bugs ready to pounce, we stripped to our underwear, climbed out onto the slimy rocks, and lost ourselves in the glimmering, thundering world that totally smashed any other sensation we happened to be entertaining. Under that waterfall, my smile blotted out everything. Nothing else mattered.

✻   ✻   ✻

Back down at the beach, while resting on the rotten hull of a half-sunk, old dugout, we were greeted by a two-kid welcome committee that came down from an unspoiled village on the hillside above. We had to venture up there and get a closer look.

The crude stone stairway up through the terraced rice paddies was steep, and above us sang a whole chorus of crazy birds. We reached the top of the hill, where we found ourselves high above the bay, nearly out of hearing range of our waterfall, and looking over at a fairytale cluster of thatched roofs. We came to something resembling a Nepali manger scene. Corn stalks, goats, and cows in a pile of hay, under a thatched roof with a glorious view of Phewa Lake and its Buddhist temple below and, on a clear day, many of the world's highest peaks.

Heading down the hill, we followed the path through the rice paddy and came to an inviting scene. Children were playing and swinging a baby in a hammock under the shade of a heavily thatched eave. An old retired Indian Army man came over and welcomed us. We had a warm conversation and heard about his battles against the Chinese when they invaded in 1962, and against Pakistan in later years. He gets a 290 rupees ($23) a month pension and is living comfortably here in his peaceful village of Anadu. We said *namaste* and made our way down to our boat. When I turned around, there were several people waving goodbye.

We shoved off and, in an extremely relaxed fashion, we half-drifted and half-paddled back past the Buddhist temple to our waiting bikes. The boat slowly drifted around, giving me a spectacular, panoramic, 360-degree view of the lake and the Pokhara Valley. I just lay there. Surrendering to the wind and the water, I let it set the tempo and show me the sights on its terms.

It was dark by the time we got back to Pokhara, returned our trusty rental bikes (they served us well during our time here) and walked back to our hotel. We were back in our room just in time for the blackout. Without electricity, it was pitch dark and in a few minutes a servant came rushing in with candles and matches for us. Without him, we would have just continued to lie there, content and in darkness, feeling good.

We passed through our flickering hallway and went down for our candlelit dinner. The flickering ambiance was made even nicer by our great Tibetan waiters—such a joy to talk and joke with. They are really wonderful people and as we learned from them, they learned from us. They taught me to say "beautiful girl": *rāmrī kēṭī*. I explained all the symbolism on the US dollar bill to them. They didn't understand why a rupee wasn't worth a dollar. I then taught them how to make a mushroom out of George Washington. Guiding their fingers, I helped them fold the bill length-wise so Washington's neck meets his forehead. Creating an American hero named Mushroom Washington brought them great joy and lots of laughter.

Knowing we were leaving tomorrow, one of them told me he would pray to the gods and goddesses of the sky for good weather.

Katmandu.

We woke up early but shouldn't have. I really
felt like getting an early start, Gene wanted a
good breakfast, nothing was open, we clumped around
not deciding anything and got a late start & a
lousy breakfast. But then the day got good

Bug guts

Follow "Pig Alley" to the "Monkey Temple"

First on our list for today was the majestic Swayambhunath Chaitya. The impressive temple on a nearby
hill overlooks all of Katmandu valley.

Passing through the ever-enchanting Durbar Square,
we had to pause to observe the morning activity and
snap a few pictures. So much was happening everywhere —
people ringing temple bells, throwing flowers, guys getting
shaves on the steps of a temple to Shiva and old ladies
picking lice out of each other's hair, I'm going through
my film too fast but around here its very hard to
cool off my trigger finger.

We entered pig Alley and stopped at "Chai & Pie"
for coffee cake, apple pie & tea and to listen to his
Bob Dylan records on a slow spinning turntable. An old
joker who claimed to be a fortune teller joined us
uninvited & started reading my palm etc. He was so
lousy he was entertaining. My lucky day is Friday, my
number is 7 and my age is 23. How about that.

Pig Alley is aptly named. We walked among the pigs &
the muck, children crapping in the streets and old people
framed in older windows. It was an interesting walk and
we passed many colorful people returning from the hill top
temple. After checking out a great temple we crossed the
Vishnumati River on an old suspension pedestrian bridge.
Then after a bizarre walk through a great neighborhood
& passing more & more people & even a small marching
band we came to the base of the hill and before
us was a long stair way lined with Buddhas, beggars
& monkeys!

This was a thrill. An old orange clad holy man
gave me bread. I fed the monkeys & we climbed &
climbed.

On top we entered a dreamy world. This 2,000 year old huge stupa and the many surrounding temples we alive, seething with worshippers who climbed this hill to throw rice light candles, burn things, paste red dots on their foreheads, spin dozens of whirling prayer wheels, mummer & mutter, and worship in other ways that I couldn't understand. So much was happening - a totally sensual experience - the cymbals, flutes, drums & chanting of the musicians, the sweet smell of flowers + incense + the constant movement. Above it all stared the all seeing eyes of Buddha and spoiled monkeys, who like cows, are a religiously favored animal. Gene + I lost ourselves on this busy summit. I wish I understood a bit more about Buddhism + Hinduism.

Before going back down we decided to enjoy the great view of Kathmandu and eat a box of Glucose biscuits. I opened the little box, took out a biscuit + like lightning, a rude but effective monkey swiped it right out of my hand! I was startled. He wanted more + frightened, I timidly tossed him another. I quickly ate one + he came at me demanding more. I stood up + began to flee but he prowled right after me. A friend joined him + I was about to be viciously double-teamed. Nervously and not wanting to be ripped to ribbons by a holy monkey I tossed him the entire box and he jumped atop a small temple +, very humanly, ate the biscuits one by one. I was totally defeated + even slightly wounded, which I will have to treat with iodine. The monkeys may be holy but they're far from clean.

We walked back down and returned to Durbar square where we intended to study our info + figure out just what everything is in this very holy maze. I could just sit in this square - I love it. We went from one pagoda temple to the next, climbing a few to check out the views and get a close look at the graphically carved erotic art all around the roofs. Incredible, explicit, and often quite kinky. This "art" was to shock the lightning god + spare the temple from a strike. Really effective apparently, because all the temples are still standing, never having been struck by lightning. I had to zoom in for a couple of X-rated pictures. After a few more studies + temples we were ready for a rest back in our hotel.

*The temples of Durbar Square
mark the center of Kathmandu.*

The Emerald City of the Hippie Trail is Kathmandu. And that was our destination today. The 30-minute warning whistle was the signal for the boy to clear the water buffalo off the pasture and get ready for an airplane. The cows on the Pokhara runway scattered. I waited under the big *peepal* tree as the plane rumbled by me on the runway. Then we climbed into the Twin Otter plane for the 30-minute flight to the finale of our journey.

The props flipped over and whirled into nothingness. The pilot released something and we jerked into motion, speeding down the grassy runway. Then we were airborne over the thatched huts, lush fields, and now tiny water buffalo. In an instant, we were soaring over the lower Himalayas. Below us slept terraced hills, scattered villages, a few brown trails and rivers—and no roads. This was real wilderness.

And then we were in Kathmandu. Reaching it, I felt like we had really accomplished something. I was psyched to turn this dream city into reality. This is the ancient capital of the Kingdom of Nepal—a land and a people that had already won a place in my heart.

We took a cab to the center of town and I got my first glimpse of its iconic pagoda-style Buddhist and Hindu temples. This is what I've always seen in guidebooks and now I'm standing before them.

We found a hotel that was more cheap than good, but it was located right on the main square—Durbar Square. I stepped out on our neat little deck and enjoyed a birds-eye view down on all the market-square-type activity spreading out below me. We unpacked, but I couldn't sit still with all those exotic temples just down the street.

I lost myself in Durbar Square. This was a tangled, medieval-ish world of tall, terraced temples; fruit and vegetable stands; thin, wild, and hungry people praying, begging, and going through rituals; children, oblivious to it all, playing tag among the frozen Buddhas; rickshaws; and bread carts. Ten years ago, the only blemishes of our modern world—cars and tourists—weren't there and the sight would have been pure. But even with long, straggly-haired, lacy, baggy-clothed freaks lounging on stony pagoda steps, and the occasional honking taxi, this was a place where I could linger. It's a living museum, a cultural circus, a story that doesn't need a plot.

Gene and I put away the guidebook and gave up trying to understand each thing, and just wandered under Buddha's ever-watching, all-knowing eyes, under monkey gods and erotic carvings, and under ornately carved temples. Holy men were holy, beggars begged, hawkers hawked, and dwarfs and hunchbacks did their thing.

We went from one pagoda temple to the next, climbing a few to check out the views and get a close look at the graphically carved erotic art all around the roofs. Incredible, explicit, and often quite kinky. This "art" was to shock the lightning god and spare the temple from a strike. Really effective, apparently, because all the temples are still standing.

Next, we had a real treat in store. We got to see Kumari Devi. Known as "the living virgin goddess," she's a young girl without zits or blemishes. When chosen she stays in the special house from the time she's five until she reaches puberty. Poor thing. After she's released, no man will marry her because as soon as someone makes love with her he will drop dead…or so the story goes. Who wants to risk that? From her balcony, she looked down at us with awe-inspiring

*Mother and child near Durbar
Square, Kathmandu.*

Could he be a once-upon-a-time New Yorker?

melancholy in her powerfully painted eyes. I caught her eye and was having a serious stare-down with the world's only living virgin goddess. Hmmm. Now that's an experience!

She vanished and I turned around to find a guy who looked like a devilish King Neptune, with long, greasy, unkempt black hair, a woven beard that hung like a heavy necklace, a tall cane, and a very "apart-from-the-world" look on his face. He was wonderfully framed in an ornate wooden doorway, and the only thing I could possibly do was take a picture. Looking through my view-finder, I studied his face. And, with a kind of double-take, I thought I saw a hint of an American tired of the rat-race who totally checked out and is well on the way to forever-matted hair and bare feet with hoof-like callouses. Could he be a once-upon-a-time New Yorker?

Then we walked into the more residential section of the city and, after a few good turns, we were deep in the world's only Nepali urban jungle. Before us opened a large square lined by old wooden buildings—and blackened with age. It was full of playing children, many flying frisky little kites.

We ducked into a side courtyard and found a neighborhood temple. Actually, it seems all houses had a courtyard and all courtyards are a religious temple of some sort. This one was quite fancy. An old man gruffly got rid of all the children, winning us peace to fully appreciate the lovely space. The Nepalis have kind of accepted both Buddhism and Hinduism and I guess their religion is a combination of both.

We wandered slowly through this other-worldly neighborhood, totally away from the tourist center. The people here seem to live to be peaceful, kind, and warm. Their bright eyes and smiles make me smile. Some cute kids followed us around. We discovered another temple with erotic art. The Nepali kids snickered knowingly as we slowly made our way around the temple, necks craned and mouths hanging open.

Nepal

Wandering deeper into Kathmandu, we paused to observe the busy slice of life scenes: people ringing temple bells, throwing flowers, guys getting shaves on the steps of the temple to Shiva, and old ladies picking lice out of each other's hair.

We continued down a street the hippies call "Pig Alley"—aptly named, it certainly has enough pigs—and stopping at a legendary (at least among hippies) eatery: Pie & Chai. Pie & Chai is the kind of shop everyone would like just down the street. Friendly atmosphere, always there with good music, fresh pie and cake, and plenty of tea.

Joining the hippie crowd, we savored delicious hot apple pie, fresh chocolate banana cake, and milky tea, while listening to Bob Dylan. What a treat. An old joker who claimed to be a fortune teller joined us uninvited and started reading my palm and predicting my future. He was so lousy he was entertaining. My lucky day is Friday, my number is seven, and my age is 23. How about that.

⁂ ⁂ ⁂

The majestic Swayambhunath Chaitya Temple sits on a nearby hill overlooking all of Kathmandu Valley.

We followed the crowds of colorful worshippers heading for the hill-capping temple. We crossed the Bishnumati River on an old pedestrian suspension bridge. Then, after walking through a great neighborhood and passing more and more people, and even a small marching band, we came to the base of the hill. Before us was a long stairway lined with Buddhas, beggars, and sacred monkeys! This was a thrill. An old orange-clad holy man gave me bread. I fed the monkeys and we climbed and climbed.

On top we entered a dreamy world. This 2,000-year-old towering stupa and the many surrounding temples were alive, seething with worshippers who climbed this hill to throw rice, light candles, burn things, paste red dots on their foreheads, spin dozens of whirling prayer wheels, murmur and mutter, and worship in other ways that

Monkeys at the Swayambhu
Complex in Kathmandu

Marijuana, called ganja in India and Nepal, is sold in the markets like an herb.

I couldn't understand. So much was happening—the cymbals, flutes, drums, and chanting of the musicians, the sweet smell of flowers and incense, and the constant movement. Above it all stared the all-seeing eyes of Buddha and spoiled monkeys who, like cows, are a religiously favored animal. Gene and I lost ourselves on this busy summit—a totally sensual experience.

Before going back down we decided to enjoy the great view of Kathmandu and treat ourselves to our last box of glucose biscuits. I opened the little box, took out a biscuit and, like lightning, a rude but effective monkey swiped it right out of my hand! I was startled. He wanted more and, frightened, I timidly tossed him another. I quickly ate one and he came at me, demanding more. I stood up and began to flee but he prowled right after me. A friend joined him and I was about to be viciously double-teamed. Nervously and not wanting to be ripped to ribbons by a holy monkey, I tossed him the entire box and he jumped atop a small temple. Very humanly, he ate my prized biscuits one by one intentionally just beyond my reach. I was totally defeated and even slightly wounded, which I will have to treat with iodine. The monkeys may be holy but they're far from clean and I can't look at a monkey's teeth without thinking rabies.

* * *

A special life flourishes in Durbar Square after dark. We relaxed out on our balcony and smoked a funny-looking cigarette of ganja, joking about our friend, Shiva the Destroyer. This was Nepali marijuana, not hashish, and, as I leaned against the balcony wall feeling the Gs of my rocket taking off, I wondered "why is this experience illegal back home." This was great—better than hash. After a few watery-eyed, smoky moments we were stepping back into the world of yak, yeti, Kumari, and Shiva.

All I wanted to do was go out and stroll among the pagodas, flutes, and sleeping dogs. The square hummed with muffled activity.

I saw things I'd never noticed before. Perfectly stoned, we wandered through dark Durbar Square. We climbed to the top of a pagoda temple and the temples around us became ducks and dogs. All those ever-present eyes of Buddha seemed determined to root out both loneliness and privacy. We got two fat little bananas and had a glorious time trying to peel those buggers. They tasted strange...and dry. Like a pot-smoking know-it-all, Gene explained, "You've got chalky mouth."

This was a good night in Kathmandu: Everything seemed to be happening. In the courtyard of "Kumari, the living virgin goddess," we found a large group of people gathered around a very animated speaker who seemed to talk forever and never slow down. We dropped by a little later and he was still going. We hung around for a while, just looking at all the people and hoping that the living goddess would make an appearance. She never came out, so we left. Gingerly, we climbed to the dizzy top of a nearby pagoda temple and found some sleeping locals. This was a good perch to observe the square, and observe we did.

We continued our walk. Three men sitting around a flame and smoking, invited us to sit cross-legged with them. Listening to Indian music (which really came alive for me), we discussed the buffer function of Nepal between India and China. The men looked like a Rembrandt as the flames flickered on their golden faces. Later, we entered a room full of intense music...churning cymbals, drums, harmonium, chanters, flutes, and worshippers. What an experience to just sit and observe!

I doubt if I want to smoke a lot of pot in the future. But I love to travel and I'm realizing that high is a place and they don't call going there a trip for nothing. While everything is vividly alive and more intense than normal, nothing seems to be real and that scares me a little. Before, I always shunned pot as a token of my self-discipline and control. Now I smoke it as an example of self-control and to widen my view of the world. I never could conceive of philosophers doubting reality or pondering another reality. Now I can see that much more exists than meets the eye.

We passed a small group of ganja-ed musicians and headed down Pig Alley back to Pie & Chai. We sat in the corner and went "Pig Alley wild." We each went through three big slices of mostly apple pie and three cups of tea. Just imagine—hot apple pie coming out of the medieval brick pizza oven, peacenik/music lover/poet/philosophers from around the world to dream out loud with, the best rock & roll from Creedence to the Doors to Dylan to the Stones, and marijuana that makes you as high as the Himalayas that surround you—a circle of peaks that corrals the experience so nothing spills. I'm not just saying this because I'm high…my Pie & Chai memories are pure happiness.

The music was very special. Either this little bakery has the greatest speakers in the world, or I've found a way to step right into the music. When you're high, the music has dimension; not only great separation but it engulfs you. It opens its arms and lets you enter. You're right there and the littlest musical things that always passed unnoticed now jump right out at you! Wow, what a wonderful key to opening up such a sensual wonderland. I will guard that key, take it home, and put it to good use there.

Yes, Pie & Chai, every hippie's favorite bakery, gave me some of the best times of my young life.

It was our last day in Nepal, and we wanted to spend it enjoying what we like most about the country: everyday life.

We decided to bike out to a village called Kirtipur. Coasting out of town, we crossed the river and came first to the impressive university. This was interesting. Right here, on this campus, was the intelligentsia and the future of a more modern Nepal. The campus cafeteria offered both cheap food and fascinating conversation. I think if I was Nepali, this is where I'd want to be.

Then we reached the town of Kirtipur. We parked our bikes to a chorus of small voices saying, "I watch bike, me bike watch." We locked them up and climbed the stone stairs into the medieval hilltop town.

I was almost in shock! My mouth hung open as before me was a perfect medieval square—it could have been Germany during the time of Martin Luther. Braids of food and spices draped the buildings, drying in the sun. People washed in the rectangular pond next to the well; the men were gathered under eaves, making music or playing cards; ladies daydreamed while spinning yarn; and children flew kites and chased wheels with sticks. Above it all an ornately carved and aged window framed grandparents and their dog. So much was going on. But everything was small and nothing dominated. It could have been a Bruegel painting.

We poked around, walking nearly every street, peeking into every medieval courtyard and folding our hands in every temple. Small

At Kathmandu, the eastern terminus
of the Hippie Trail, backpackers gather.

Kathmandu cityscape

industry was grinding away…everywhere. This place is a lot quieter than Kathmandu and somehow it seems as if the people are different. Maybe they just don't know tourism. This town was completely untouched and pure. It's how I wish Europe was.

Today was Lord Krishna's birthday and we headed a couple miles east for Patan to celebrate. Patan is a special city: more Buddhist than Kathmandu, it used to be an independent country. First, we found its famous monastery for a look at prayer wheels, big bells, fiery dragon-type things, flowers, and Buddhas—so golden, serene, and extra large. It all seemed to remind us that China was just over the mountains.

Next, we left Buddha for the Hindu Krishna temple. We dove into the crowds of colorfully-dressed Hindus who were here for the birthday festivities. They mobbed the temple, and a line of women with offerings of gifts, 200 yards long, snaked down the street. There was energy here on this special day and the few wide-eyed tourists were quite enthralled by it all.

Then we saw lots of police and what seemed like troops of Boy Scouts clearing the road and the square, as people were gathering on the curbs for what looked like a parade. We grabbed a good place and waited. We didn't really know what for, but we waited. Finally, someone told me the King and Queen were coming. King Birendra was a young, pudgy, Harvard-educated monarch, who wore glasses like I had in sixth grade. Basically accepted by all but the college liberals, who were quite trivial in number, his passage was an occasion for a crowd, lots of police, and a long wait.

We waited and waited. My camera was set up and ready and it got darker and darker, until I ran out of f-stops and photography became hopeless. After an hour or so, we joined a row of tourists who, for some reason, were allowed special front-row seats and we waited longer.

Then the crowd rose to its feet and, with a flashing red-light escort, the king sped by, not even acknowledging the crowd that had waited nearly three hours to get a glimpse of his royal face. He disappeared into the Krishna temple and worshipped as the press flashed pictures. Then, back in his fancy car, he zoomed away. Quite a disappointment. He could have at least waved.

We *namaste-d* our way through the long, narrow village, following it up a ridge to the highest spot around. Another temple crowned this hill and from here we joined the locals admiring the pastoral view of Kathmandu Valley, which stretched out before us.

We had "done" the Hippie Trail. Looking out over its Promised Land, I told Gene I can't remember ever being more content, happy, and at such peace.

Back in Kathmandu, we returned to our hotel, and packed. Getting everything I had purchased into my rucksack was a challenge and I had to work at it. Organizing, rolling, and zipping everything up, those last-night-of-a-trip feelings set in. I'm thankful for the whole package—stumbles, frustrations, hard lessons, eurekas, joys and memories. I'm mindful that you can't see experiences on a stage. You need to earn them…to really live them. And having completed our trip—even though I expect to look back decades from now and consider this the best trip of my lifetime—going home is a celebration. Yes, I was happily packed up—with enough souvenirs for a Rudyard Kipling Christmas—and ready to fly home.

⁂ ⁂ ⁂

But I needed one last walk through old Kathmandu…alone. Anticipating a kind of a sad and reverse culture shock with tomorrow's homecoming, I wandered…slowly soaking it all in one more time. The silence in the shadows of timeless pagodas. The trance-like music of the ganja-passing musicians, with people held captive by the pull of the ringing cymbals. Dark, muddy streets with shadow

Waiting...waiting...waiting for the king.

*Throughout Nepal, even the
smallest kids greeted travelers on
the Hippie Trail with folded hands
saying "namaste." (The peace within my
soul recognizes the peace within yours.)*

dogs lurking and silent pools of water. Stone lions in pairs coming to life with each passing headlight.

For some reason, in Kathmandu, I never worked to get truly oriented. Following my nose, I still got myself turned around in this urban dream-scape: snotty-nosed kids crying in doorways, straw mats covered with drying peppers, and lounging cows. Paint-smeared faces appeared on both people and their stony gods, and kids with raggy shirts ran around bottomless. A little boy peeing in the street ran after a dog before he was through. A lady with seven rings in each ear calmed her child by nursing her while singing softly.

I went down Pig Alley and, of course, had to have one last stop at Pie & Chai. The sloping, pie-filled room was full of freaks doing time in Kathmandu. A Frenchman who looked like Richelieu with long curly hair played chess, and an intellectual-looking guy with John Lennon glasses didn't read his book over in the corner. They had broken the bonds of "back home."

I treated myself to one last jumbo slice of apple pie and tea with a lovely Rolling Stones serenade. For me, being on the road usually means being away from my favorite music. Pie & Chai brings it together.

I concentrated on my pie and the music—and the impossibility of sustaining this wonder after stepping onto that plane tomorrow—while half-heartedly playing a game of chess across from a German girl. I traded queens, paid my 3 rupees, and stepped back into the streets.

It was pitch black by the time I entered my hotel. The candle-light made Buddha glimmer and shine on the lobby floor. The desk boy was sleeping when I passed. And I went to bed thinking about tomorrow...and home.

Awaiting our plane under the peepal tree at the Pokhara airport.

WELCOME TO POKHARA!

Transportation statistics—

Frankfurt – Beograd –	23 hrs	train	$80
Beograd – Sofia	10 hrs	train	$16
Sofia – Istanbul	15 hrs	train	$16
Istanbul – Tehran	63 hrs	bus	$32

    actual time w/ accident – 4 nights + 3 days.

Tehran – Mashad	18 hrs	bus	$6
Mashad – Border of Afganistan	3 hrs	bus	$2
Iran – Afgan border	5 hours		
Border – Herat	3½ hours	bus	$1.50
Herat – Kabul	14 hour	bus	$5

    Qadafi bus co. = great

Kabul – Peshawar	8 hours	bus	$2.50

    Pakistan Bus Co. – good
    includes 3 hours at border

Peshawar – Lahore	12 hours	train	$3.50

    1st class $3.50 2nd class $2
    we broke trip to sleep in Rawalpindi

Lahore – Amritsar	4 hours	bus or taxi	$1

    including 2 hours at the border

Total Frankfurt – India (Amritsar) $165
    about 180 hours including
    border + other hassles

Amritsar – Jammu	7 hours	train	$1 2nd class / $5 1st class sleeper
Jammu – Srinagar	12 hours	bus	$2.50
Srinagar – Delhi	1 hour	plane	$30
Delhi – Gorpakhan	1 hour	plane	27
Tansen – Pokara	6 hours	bus	$1.50
Pokara – Katmandu	½ hour	plane	$10
Katmandu – Patna	1 hour	plane	$20
Patna – Varanasi	5 hours	train	1.50 2nd class
Varanasi – Agra	13 hours	train	4.00 2nd cl. sleeper
Agra – Jaipur	8 hours	train	2.00 2nd cl sleeper
Jaipur – Delhi	6 hours	bus + truck	$1.50
Delhi – London	12 hours	plane	$340 Thai budget fare.
London – Frankft	13 hours	train	$40 to

Accomodations—   Price for double
                                                                  (w/o food)

July 14   Train   Munich → Yugoslavia   ═══
     15   Beograd   sleep in train station   ═══
     16,17 Plovdiv   suetis   ═══
     18   Train   Plovdiv → Istanbul
     19   Istanbul   Hotel Agan   175 lira $7
     20   Bus   Istanbul → Erzurum
     21   Middle of Turkey, 5 hours in lousy hotel, 30 lira $7.40
     22   Erzurum   lousy hotel   35 lira $2.80
     23   Bus   long night
     24   Teheran   Tourist Hotel Amir Kabir A hole!   6.00
     25,26 Teheran   Abes place - great guy.   3.00
     27,28 Mashad   campground, great swimming pool
     29,30,31 Herat Mowafaq Hotel - 1st class $5.00
                      great food pool, friendly, clean
                      central location 200 afs $3.80

August 1,2,3 Kabul Sina Hotel - next to Mustafa
                      hotel near chicken street. quiet
                      friendly, nice courtyard w b-fast
     4   Rawalpindi A no name flop house $1.00
     5   Lahore   Hotel Menora - 41 Mcleod Rd   6.50
                      Phone- 56188   great, friendly,
                      with private shower WC + fan
                      across from Hotel Lahore, central
     6   Train   Amritsar → Jammu   ═══
     7,8,9,13 Srinagar Muzaffer Houseboat 80 rs ($10) for   4.00
                      double, full board + complete service.
     10   Gulmarg   Kingsley Hotel - very nice   2.50
     11,12 Lake Nagin "The Ritz" houseboat, Truely delux   5.00
                      $6 each for 3 meals, great servants + peace
     14,15,16,17 Delhi YMCA Jai Singh St. 43 rs 6×6 each   8.00
     18   Tansen   Siddhartha Hotel - the nicest available   1.50
     19,20,21 Pokara Hotel Mount Annapurna, the best   11.00
                      place so far - totally first class with
                      great restaurant,
     22,23,24,25 Katmandu Sugat Hotel, Basantapur Square   4.00
     26,27 Varanasi Hotel International, big clean +   8.00
                      air conditioned. Not great but OK
     28   Train   Varanasi → Agra   ═══
     29   Agra   Grand Hotel 75 rs for A/c B+B   7.00
                      Air Cond. Good cheap restaurant, great
                      service, room, bath + location
     30   Train + Jaipur IInd class sleeper + Tourist Bungalo   2.00
     31   Jaipur   Khetri House, B+B 77rs   6.50
                      Fantastic stately living Maharashtan palace
Sept 1,2,3 Delhi   YMCA Jai Singh St.   8.00
     4   Plane   flying over Asia   ═══
     5,6 London   The Szpet's house   ═══

Postscript

Although we didn't know it at the time, 1978 was the final summer of the Hippie Trail. With the Soviet invasion of Afghanistan and the Islamic revolution in Iran, safe and easy travel through both countries came to an abrupt end in 1979.

People have told me, wistfully, that they wish this trip could still be done and that the Hippie Trail experience is gone now...a casualty of our modern and globalized world. I disagree. This trip was not Iran, Afghanistan, and India in 1978. It was a 23-year-old on the verge of adulthood, getting to know the world.

That same world and those same 23-year-olds are still out there. I frequently hear from young globetrotters who have ventured beyond "tourism" to become friends with the world, and I'm inspired by their stories.

I believe anyone—even in these "have a safe trip" days—can still stow away on the Reality Express like Gene and I did, get their fingers dirty in other cultures, wallop their ethnocentrism, and come home with the most valuable souvenir: a broader perspective.

I miss the days of "bon voyage." There's so much fear these days. But the flip side of fear is understanding, and we gain understanding through travel. Travelers learn that fear is for people who don't get out much; that culture shock is the growing pains of that broadening perspective; that we're all children of God—and by traveling, we get to know the family.

In my work, I've shared the lessons I learned on the Hippie Trail for over 40 years. And I'm an evangelist for the notion that good travel is more than bucket lists and selfies.

I believe that if more people could have such a transformative experience—especially in their youth—our world would be a more just and stable place. Travelers understand that the big challenges of the future will be blind to borders, and we'll need to tackle them together—as global citizens and as a family of nations. And most fundamentally, travelers know that the world is a welcoming place filled with joy, love, and good people.

Young or old, rich or poor, backpack or rolling suitcase, the best way to understand this is to experience it firsthand. To get out there and get to know our neighbors. To build not walls, but bridges.

I penned 60,000 words on the Hippie Trail, then flew home and dove into adulthood. In the wake of this adventure—having stoked my travel spirit—I made a decision that changed the trajectory of my life: I let my piano students go, turned my recital hall into a lecture hall, and began a small travel business.

Keep on travelin'

Rick Steves

Rick and Gene homeward bound.
(To read a digital scan of Rick's
original hand-written journal,
go to ricksteves.com/hippietrail.)